The Role of Commissions in Policy-Making

A Royal Institute of Public Administration study

Public Inquiries as an Instrument of Government
by R. E. Wraith and G. B. Lamb

The Role of Commissions in Policy-Making

EDITED BY RICHARD A. CHAPMAN
Reader in Politics, University of Durham

LONDON. GEORGE ALLEN & UNWIN LTD
Ruskin House   Museum Street

ISBN 0 04 350042 0 Hardback
     0 04 350043 9 Paperback

Printed in Great Britain
in 10 *point Plantin type*
by Clarke, Doble & Brendon Ltd
Plymouth

Contents

1 Introduction

RICHARD A. CHAPMAN

In British central government there are several terms signifying categories of *ad hoc* advisory body. This can be confusing if people do not appreciate that, although particular institutions may be called, for example, Royal Commissions, Commissions, Committees, or Working Parties, there is in practice little difference between them.

Commissions, as used in the title of this book, is a group term for the bodies presided over by Fulton, Plowden, Donovan, Redcliffe-Maud and Seebohm, because they may together be seen as falling within the fairly narrow categories, suggested by K. C. Wheare,* of committees to advise and inquire. When used in this way a commission may be defined as a body set up by a government to consider a specific problem or problems. It works within fairly clearly indicated constraints of time, resources and, in particular, the political environment. It may have a party political role which, when present, is concealed as far as possible behind a neutral façade.

This book is an attempt to draw attention to some of the common and contrasting features of five commissions and to advance some suggestions that may help future commissions to be more useful. The five commissions were chosen partly because they operated within a short period of time when there was considerable concern in Britain for reforming our public institutions, and partly because five university teachers with special interests in these particular bodies felt that it might be useful to analyse them using a common frame of reference.

Each contributor has had a close interest in the work of his chosen commission. We have all, for several years, been lecturing and writing about problems of administration in the areas studied by the commissions – in addition Maurice Kogan had a rather different relationship to his commission for he was Secretary to the Plowden Committee.

At the beginning we agreed on a scheme of analysis which each has tried to follow in his chapter, but this has not been easy for, as we worked, we soon discovered that the features we had in mind were of

* K. C. Wheare, *Government by Committee*, OUP, 1955.

different significance in relation to the various commissions. We have
been as frankly critical as possible, and perhaps this should be borne in
mind where we have submitted reports to a degree of textual analysis
which their writers never intended: we feel such analysis is not unreasonable, though we have also drawn attention, as far as possible, to
the constraints under which those responsible were working. It has been
difficult to make generalisations from so small a sample, but we have
taken some hesitant steps in the belief that policy-making studies have
to begin somewhere and these commissions and our willingness to make
the attempt seemed too good an opportunity to miss.

We have all incurred debts in writing our essays and for various
reasons have not been able to acknowledge fully all the help we have
received – in several cases from officials to whom we are particularly
grateful. However, each contributor is alone responsible for his chapter
and we particularly do not wish those we have thanked to feel they are
associated in any way with our views or the analysis we have pursued.
We are very grateful to Miss Janet Howe for making the index and
helping with the proofs.

2 The Fulton Committee on the Civil Service

RICHARD A. CHAPMAN*

BACKGROUND AND PRE-HISTORY TO THE COMMITTEE

Towards the mid nineteen-sixties there was a spate of introspective books and articles critically analysing various British institutions and calling for modernisation; but the Civil Service, for long the subject of music-hall jokes, was the target for attack of a more consistently academic origin than other institutions.

One of the first and most significant publications in the pre-Fulton decade to criticise the Civil Service in a stimulating way was the essay by Thomas Balogh (now Lord Balogh) entitled 'The Apotheosis of the Dilettante', published in *The Establishment*, a symposium edited by Hugh Thomas.[1] Balogh criticised the Service for being 'the establishment of mandarins' and found its basic weakness in its structure which, he said, favoured centralisation and dilettantism. Following that essay the next critical piece of writing to make a similar impact was Brian Chapman's *British Government Observed* in which the author explained his contention 'that the source of many of our present ills is institutional, and lies in a mistaken veneration for old ideas, and a refusal to examine them coolly and objectively'.[2]

However, in terms of pre-history to the Fulton Committee the Fabian Tract, *The Administrators*,[3] is particularly notable. Written by a group of Fabians (the Chairman was Mr R. R. Neild, subsequently a member of the Fulton Committee, and the group also included Mrs Shirley Williams and Lord Balogh; in addition some civil servants are believed to have taken part in the work) interested in the reform of the higher Civil Service, it has a number of basic similarities with the scope, approach, and style of presentation of the Fulton Report. The pamphlet was not about the Civil Service as a whole but about the Administrative

* I wish to thank for their most helpful comments on an earlier draft of this essay Dame Enid Russell-Smith, Dr J. F. Pickering, Mr R. W. L. Wilding and Mr R. J. Williams.

Class, 'the governing class in the Service', and those members of the professional class of roughly equivalent status. It said: 'The scope of government responsibility in the field of economic and social policy has greatly increased since the war and is likely to continue to increase. But the Civil Service has not changed to meet those new responsibilities . . . The system is plainly out of touch with the times, being unfitted to more positive government. . . . Our criticism is focussed on three main characteristics of the system: (a) Amateurism, resulting from the all-rounder tradition and from the tradition that the administrator on the job is the best adviser on policy; (b) The tendency for civil servants to be too secretive in their approach, concentrating on procedure and on the day-to-day dispatch of paper rather than on the substance of problems, and being too ready to seek compromises; (c) The tendency to be too closed and secretive in the formulations of policy . . . Our general aim is to make the Civil Service more professional, more adaptable to new methods and more creative in fulfilling new tasks. The main methods which we propose are wider recruitment, better training and more movement in and out of the service; the fuller use of experts, the improvement of the status of professionals *vis-à-vis* general administrators, and in some instances an increase in their numbers; and the explicit acceptance of the need for more political appointments.' One of the most interesting points of style is reflected in the phrase 'blocks of work' – not a phrase which particularly stands out when *The Administrators* alone is read; but it is worth noting after reading the Fulton Report where it occurs much more frequently.

About the same time, in 1964, Harold Wilson was interviewed by Norman Hunt for the BBC and asked about his plans for the modernisation of Britain. He explained that he was worried about what he felt was the amateurism of the central direction of Government and he outlined reforms he had in mind if he won the general election – including the better use of experts, more transfers into and out of the Civil Service and a strengthened Cabinet Secretariat.[4] The Labour Party manifesto for the 1964 general election contained similar sentiments and said that the root of the country's problems for the previous thirteen years had been 'A Philosophy of the Past'; this would be rectified by a Labour government which would 'make government more efficient. As the tasks of government grow more numerous and more complex the machinery of government must be modernised. . . .'[5]

However, the main pre-cursor to the Fulton Report was obviously the 'Recruitment to the Civil Service' Report of the Select Committee on Estimates, published in August 1965.[6] Included in its recommendations was the proposal that 'A Committee . . . should be appointed to initiate research upon, to examine, and to report upon the structure, recruitment and management of the Civil Service'. That recommendation was accepted by the Government and on 8 February 1966 Mr Harold Wilson, then Prime Minister, announced in the House of Commons the appointment of the Fulton Committee 'to examine the structure, recruitment and management, including training, of the Home Civil Service, and to make recommendations'.[7]

Because of the growing attitude critical of public institutions it was not an entirely unexpected decision that a committee would be established at that time. It had almost become an accepted convention that there would be a major inquiry into the Civil Service about once in every generation of civil servants: since the beginning of the century the MacDonnell Royal Commission had reported in 1914, the Tomlin Royal Commission in 1931, and the Priestley Royal Commission in 1955, though the latter was less wide-ranging in the scope of its inquiries. The climate of self-examination in the country at large was reflected in the political system where, in some instances, it overrode party political considerations – for example, the Maud and Mallaby Committees to consider management and staffing in local government had already been set up before the Conservative government went out of office in 1964. So it is quite possible that had the Conservatives remained in office they may have instituted an inquiry into some aspects of the Service, though the form the inquiry would have taken, and the terms of reference and membership of the committee would have been very different.

It should be noted that the Fulton inquiry was the work of a departmental committee and not a Royal Commission, and to some people this was significant. It meant that the Fulton exercise had a number of advantages and disadvantages which put it in a rather different category from preceding Royal Commissions on the Civil Service, though they may have had similarly wide terms of reference. Whilst a departmental committee does not appear to enjoy the same kind of formal authority and prestige as a Royal Commission it was expected to work more quickly, and it was thought that individuals who gave evidence might speak more freely if the Committee chose (as it did) not to publish the minutes of oral evidence (though it should, perhaps, also be added that not all Royal Commissions have published all the evidence they received). In the Civil Service inquiry it was believed that these advantages might be especially appreciated by officials, accustomed to working within the constraints of the doctrine of ministerial responsibility, who might feel able to be more critical of the system in which they worked than if they had been giving evidence publicly before a Royal Commission. Also, the presence of civil servants on the Committee might have been expected to make its recommendations more acceptable within the Service. Moreover, as Sir Laurence Helsby explained to the Select Committee on Estimates in 1965: 'There is a great advantage . . . in having a review of the Service undertaken by a group of people, some of whom at any rate have had direct experience of how the machine works, and what it feels like to be part of it, and that you lose if you have a Royal Commission when by tradition no civil servant will be a member of it.' However, *post-hoc* analysis of the proceedings of the Fulton Committee is hampered somewhat because, with such a departmental committee it is more difficult to discover whose ideas the Committee accepted, which evidence was most highly valued, and how the members of the Committee reacted when evidence was being given.

Within the Service there had also been a degree of criticism as well as significant reforms. Civil Servants, always wary of the Treasury, were increasingly restless about the management divisions which had never assumed a very active central management role or devoted sufficient resources to it, and which seemed to have little interest in the career management of scientists, engineers, accountants and lawyers. There had also been important innovations in the nineteen-sixties: for example, the Treasury Centre for Administrative Studies was established in 1963, following the recommendations of the Morton Committee – an interdepartmental committee set up in 1962 under the chairmanship of Mr (now Sir) Wilfred Morton. Its first intake, in 1963, was no more than experimental, and consisted of fifty-eight civil servants of one age from a single class. Indeed, the three years from 1963 to 1966 have been regarded by Desmond Keeling,[8] former Director of Training in the Treasury, as a period of experiment, whereas he regarded the period from 1966 to 1970 as one of expansion. So the Fulton Committee was conducting its inquiries at an opportune time for independent appraisal of the CAS, when there was already criticism of the Treasury, and when civil servants, rarely insensitive to public criticism, were likely to be sympathetic.

The setting up of the Fulton Committee was generally greeted with approval. Whilst *The Economist*[9] did not actually say it welcomed the setting up of the Committee, it certainly did not give it the cold shoulder; in a second leading article it published 'Some Comments for the attention of the new Fulton Committee'. A leading article in *The Guardian* (9 February 1966) called the Fulton Committee 'a small, expert, workmanlike group'; and on the same day *The Times* referred to the timeliness of the inquiry announced by the Prime Minister. Similar reactions were expressed by Civil Service staff associations. For example, the Civil Service Clerical Association welcomed the inquiry and made a number of fundamental criticisms of the Service indicating the sort of issue it hoped the Committee would examine: it said, for example: 'The CSCA is convinced that the present grading structure, laid down in 1920 and virtually unchanged since, is unsuitable for the totally different conditions of the Civil Service and the community it serves.'[10] The General Secretary of the Society of Civil Servants referred to the Fulton Committee as 'lively' and much of the issue of *Civil Service Opinion* for March 1966 was devoted to analysing the problems it was hoped the Committee would review.

The Fulton Committee comprised the folowing twelve members:

Lord Fulton (Chairman)	(Vice-Chancellor, University of Sussex)
Sir Norman Kipping	(former head of the Federation of British Industries)
Sir Philip Allen	(Second Secretary, HM Treasury; Permanent Under-Secretary of State, Home Office, since 1966)
Mr W. C. Anderson	(General Secretary, National and Local Government Officers Association)
Rt Hon. Sir Edward Boyle MP	(former Minister of Education)
Sir William Cook	(Chief Scientific Adviser to the Ministry of Defence)
Sir James Dunnett	(Permanent Secretary to the Ministry of Labour; Permanent Under-Secretary of State, Ministry of Defence, since 1966)
Dr Norman Hunt	(Fellow of Exeter College, Oxford)
Mr R. R. Neild	(Economic Adviser to HM Treasury)
Mr R. Sheldon MP	(who, in April 1966, succeeded Mrs Shirley Williams MP on her appointment as Parliamentary Secretary, Ministry of Labour)
Professor Lord Simey	(Professor of Social Science, University of Liverpool)
Sir John Wall	(Managing Director, Electrical and Musical Industries Ltd.)

It is not easy to know why these particular people were appointed. *The Economist*, 12 February 1966, referred to them as 'three dons, four very able top civil servants (at least three of them rather unconventional), two extremely intelligent MPs, two leading industrialists, and the statutory white collar trade unionist'. The Official Secrets Acts preclude access to files at this early date to discover further reasoning behind the selection, and in any case this could well be a topic of personal or political embarrassment. But it is obvious that the Permanent Head of the Civil Service, then Sir Lawrence Helsby, advised the Prime Minister on the appointments, especially the appointment of the civil servants, and all three academics were from social science disciplines (though none was at the time noted for specialising in public administration) and known to be sympathetic to the Labour Party. Clearly, the Committee members had also to be acceptable to both the Prime Minister and Lord Fulton.

It is quite likely that other civil servants, such as the Secretary to the Cabinet, were consulted about the Committee membership – files in the Public Records Office[11] suggest that before the establishment of the Tomlin enquiry there was a meeting (on 19 July 1929) arranged by Sir Russell Scott, Controller of Establishments at the Treasury, to discuss who should be members of the 1929–31 Royal Commission on the Civil Service. For that inquiry Philip Snowden, then Chancellor of the Exchequer, appears to have been mainly responsible for selecting the members and his list was later approved by J. Ramsay MacDonald, the Prime Minister; at Lord Tomlin's suggestion an additional name, Sir Henry Sharp, was added to the Commission.

It is also obvious that in 1966 the type of inquiry and timing of its creation were, if not decided, at least influenced by Helsby – in 1965 he explained to the Estimates Committee the advantages of not having a Royal Commission and suggested that it would be wise to wait for at least a year so that changes then taking place could settle down ('one does not want to take the risk, I think, of false assessment of what is temporary and what is permanent').

METHOD OF WORKING

The Report is hardly an example of the elegant use of modern English, nor is its content uncontroversial; as D. N. Chester has commented: 'It bears the marks of haste, being somewhat repetitive and in parts not wholly clear.'[12] But when one bears in mind the constraints within which the Committee was working and the fact that, even with an able secretariat, all such committee reports are the results of compromises, the Report was really rather remarkable for its high quality. As Dr Johnson said in another context when referring to women's preaching, it 'is like a dog's walking on his hinder legs. It is not done well; but you are surprised to find it done at all'.[13] In fact, the members of the Committee claim to have reached a very wide measure of agreement and all signed the Report – Lord Simey, however, wrote a powerful reservation to the first chapter which contains the Committee's picture of 'The Civil Service Today'; there were also nine other reservations or statements of disagreement in footnotes in the Report.

As usual with Royal Commissions and Committees, most of its members were part-time (which, as they held such important positions, meant they had very heavy work burdens and their work for the Committee had in some cases to be squeezed into only one day a week); Norman Hunt, however, was released for over a year from his duties as Fellow of Exeter College, Oxford, so that he could devote his whole time to the work of the Committee. The Committee also had the full-time services of a Secretary and Assistant Secretary, both drawn from the Administrative Class, together with some supporting staff. The Report itself was drafted by Norman Hunt, together with Mr R. W. L. Wilding, the Committee's Secretary.

Its main method of working was the traditional one adopted by such bodies in Britain. It encouraged the submission of evidence from individuals and interested bodies, and the Committee published a large number, but not all, of the memoranda submitted to it. It also sponsored six research projects conducted by several academics and a management consultancy team – the Fulton Committee was, in fact, the first Committee or Royal Commission investigating the British Civil Service to commission research by persons outside the Service; and it also stimulated a number of government departments to produce evidence on topics the Committee felt would be relevant to its discussions.

Indeed, one of the most useful by-products of the Fulton exercise is contained in its Volume IV (Factual, Statistical and Explanatory Papers). That volume contains a vast amount of material – probably the largest assembly of factual information about the British Civil Service that has ever been published. The main document, an introductory factual memorandum, was produced early in the Committee's deliberations by the Treasury: the Treasury and other departments also later produced a large number of specific papers on matters under consideration by the Committee (e.g. 'Computers and the size of the Civil Service', 'Recruitment of Women to the Civil Service', 'Retirement Policy', 'ADP in the Civil Service'). It is the sort of material subsequent researchers are grateful for, but there is little evidence that the Committee was itself greatly influenced by it.

This method of working may be criticised for being neither purely traditional, in the sense of the Committee sitting to receive evidence only from interested bodies who wished to present it, nor high powered from an academic standpoint. Some critics have considered it unfortunate that the Committee did not at the outset appoint a Director of

Research in the manner followed by, for example, the Redcliffe-Maud Royal Commission; instead the research activities were directed and co-ordinated by the Secretariat and Norman Hunt.

Again, it is remarkable that the research turned out as well as it did. Neither the Secretary nor the Assistant Secretary was a graduate in a social science discipline, and whilst they had the necessary knowledge (and contacts) about the working of the Civil Service, they had no previous experience of the comparative literature or of directing academic research. Norman Hunt was similarly not, on appointment to the Committee, active in modern approaches to the study of public administration as his field of primary academic interest had, up to that time, been political history. The probable reasons for these research difficulties appear to be twofold. The Committee did not appoint a director of research partly because there were three academics on the Committee who might have been expected to oversee research activities (that one of them could do this full-time was due to the generosity of Exeter College), but partly also because of the pressure of time imposed by the political environment.

It is well known that the Prime Minister wanted the Committee to work as quickly as possible so that some impression could be made, and be publicly seen, in reforming the government bureaucracy. Consequently, worthwhile research activities had to be fitted into an almost impossibly tight time schedule. For example, the research for 'Profile of a Profession: the Administrative Class of the Civil Service', was commissioned during the summer of 1966 on the understanding that the resulting report could be submitted to the Committee by the end of February 1967 (in late 1966 it was still hoped that the Committee's report would be published before the end of 1967) – and even an optimistic academic could not reasonably expect to conduct a large piece of research and produce a comprehensive report within that time-scale, working on his own with no time off from his normal administrative and teaching duties in a university a couple of hundred miles from London. As with so much other academic research, the usefulness of that sponsored by the Fulton Committee was affected fundamentally by the constraints imposed on the researchers.

Some of those involved with the research were disappointed at the apparent lack of interest from the Committee. Whilst the Secretariat and Norman Hunt regularly made encouraging and sympathetic noises and gave as much assistance as possible, it was, perhaps, unfortunate that those who had done the commissioned research were never invited to meet the Committee to answer questions or elaborate on aspects that for various reasons they had been unable to present in written form with as much detail as they would have wished. When it is also remembered that the 'Social Survey of the Civil Service' was presented so late that it was published over a year after the Report of the Fulton Committee, there is reason to wonder how useful for their deliberations the Committee members considered the sponsored research, and how closely the Committee members read the research documents prepared for them. Furthermore, some at least of the research workers, aware of the attitude in official circles at the time, doubted whether any academic research would have been done at all, had it not been for the interest of Lord Simey, the enthusiasm of Norman Hunt, and the sympathy of the Secretariat.

It will be interesting, in the course of time, to learn how much money was spent on the various pieces of research (including the more demanding aspects of the Management Consultancy Group and the Social Survey – though it should be noted that the latter received valuable help, probably uncosted, from the Government Social Survey). Unfortunately, this is the type of information that will not be available until there is public access to the files in about another twenty-five years; but when it is available there could well be surprise that the cost of most of the research was so little. Furthermore, much of the cost may have been recovered by the government from sales of the Report – 32,000 copies had been printed by November 1971.[14]

Clearly, the official bureaucracy played a considerable role in the scope and manner of the research, as well as in the presentation of various departmental viewpoints. For example, the Treasury had close contact with the work of the Committee both formally (the Committee met in Treasury buildings and received much help from Treasury officials, especially the Pay and Management Group of the Treasury), and informally because so many of the Treasury officials were known to the Secretariat. There is nothing sinister or unusual about this, it is simply the way work progresses in the Service, and reflects the use of minimum resources to maximum advantage to achieve specified objectives within burdensome time constraints imposed by the political environment.

The whole exercise might, of course, have been quite different at a different time or with different personnel; but again, it should be recognised that the people selected to sit on such a government committee would not have been there had they been either unwilling to work within such constraints or unsympathetic to the overall objective of the exercise.

Similarly, only limited criticism can be levelled at the academics responsible for the research. The question that was often uppermost in their minds was whether to undertake a piece of research that was not wholly satisfactory but which might be modestly useful, or to adopt a perfectionist frame of mind and deny a possibly unique opportunity. In general, they were guided by these constraints to limit the scope of their work and to attempt something that was not academically unworthy and did shed light on the problem being considered by the Committee.

The Management Consultancy Investigation commissioned by the Committee was headed by Norman Hunt, with a civil servant from the Treasury, a management consultant, and a specialist from British Petroleum Limited. Between October 1966 and April 1967 it investigated twenty-three blocks of work in government departments, selected to provide as good a cross-section of the work done by civil servants in the general service classes as could be examined by a small team in a reasonably short time. Twelve departments provided facilities for the examination of their work, the staff associations encouraged their members to co-operate, and nearly 600 individual civil servants took part in interviews and helped in other ways. By Norman Hunt's own admission the inadequacies of the Civil Service expounded in Chapter 1 of the Report were based for the most part on the Management Consultancy Group's investigations.[15]

The Social Survey commissioned by the Committee was by postal questionnaire designed to provide the outline of a sociological portrait of the main general classes of the Civil Service. It was conducted by Dr A. H. Halsey, Head of the Department of Social and Administrative Studies at the University of Oxford, and Mr I. M. Crewe, Assistant Lecturer in Politics at the University of Lancaster; they were assisted by the Government Social Survey and the Treasury. Because the time available for the research was so short the survey was confined to factual information about the social and educational background of the sample.

The other four research projects commissioned by the Committee were conducted by particular individuals. Dr Richard A. Chapman, of Liverpool University, was commissioned to conduct a survey by questionnaire and interview of those men and women who entered the Administrative Class as Assistant Principals in 1956. Dr J. F. Pickering, of Sussex University, conducted a survey by postal questionnaire designed to examine the subsequent careers of candidates who had been unsuccessful in the open competitions for the Administrative Class fifteen years previously. Dr E. Anstey, of the Civil Service Commission, conducted a follow-up survey of members of the Administrative Class to compare the relative progress and performance of different types of entrant and to check the validity of the selection procedure. And Dr J. B. Bourn, of the Ministry of Defence, made a study of the work of the main Royal Commissions and committees that have examined the Civil Service.

The Committee itself, or members of it, made a number of visits to inform themselves of the situation elsewhere. For example, five of the twelve members of the Committee visited France from 7 to 10 November 1966, seven members of the Committee visited Sweden from 6 to 9 February 1967, and two members spent five days in Washington in September 1966. Such short trips abroad seem to have influenced the Committee's thinking as reflected in the Report, but an outside observer may wonder how firm a grasp the Committee actually had of the experience of foreign countries.

It has been stated that the Committee was struck by the remarkable consensus of opinion in the written evidence presented. 'Many tributes have been paid to the strong qualities of the Civil Service. At the same time there is a large measure of agreement on the major problems that now need to be solved and on some of the reforms that should be introduced for this purpose.'[16] How this was achieved may be seen by examining examples of evidence on selected topics.

On classification, the Treasury proposed the merger of the Administrative and Executive Classes and the formation of an integrated structure at the top of the Service down to the salary level of the maximum of the Assistant Secretary scale; the CSCA proposed the addition of the Clerical Classes to the merger proposed by the Treasury; the Treasury agreed. The IPCS proposed similar mergers of the Scientific and of the Professional (Works Group) and Technical Classes into a Science Group and a Technology Group respectively, and later the creation of a Social Scientist Group; the Treasury disagreed. The IPCS also proposed that the integrated structure at the top of the Service should be extended downwards to the maximum of the Principal scale. The First Division Association supported the merger of the Administrative and Executive Classes, but opposed the integrated group structure. Other staff associations made proposals relating to their particular parts of the Service, those representing departmental classes were for the most part strongly in favour of their preservation.

On recruitment, the Treasury proposed a wider graduate entry to administrative work, the Civil Service Commission described its procedures and suggested a method of selection for a wider graduate entry, and there were substantial comments by the staff associations and a number of individuals.

Detailed proposals on management training were made in the Report from a Treasury Working Party under the chairmanship of Mr S. P. Osmond; this was supplemented by other papers from the Treasury and staff associations and from a number of individuals and organisations including the Labour Party and the Liberal Party. Professor P. J. O.

Self (Professor of Public Administration, University of London) discussed in some detail the idea of a Civil Service College. This was also proposed by the Labour Party and Mr T. Smith (on behalf of the Acton Society Trust). The greater specialisation of administrative staff was discussed by a number of individuals, the Labour Party, and the Royal Institute of Public Administration.

The need for clear allocation of responsibility and authority was discussed by several organisations outside the Service which made recommendations for setting up integrated hierarchies and mixed teams. Stress was also laid, by such bodies as the British Institute of Management, on the importance of new management techniques, and on the need for internal efficiency audit.

The role of the Permanent Secretary was discussed in several submissions of evidence; some papers, such as those from the CBI, *The Guardian* and BEA also discussed the question of 'hiving-off' executive functions to autonomous bodies. There were very few suggestions that the Civil Service should cease to be a career service; very many that there should be more mobility and better contacts between the Service and the outside world. More late entry was recommended by the Confederation of British Industry, the Royal Society, the British Institute of Management, and some individuals.

On central management of the Civil Service, Sir Laurence Helsby, then Head of the Civil Service, presented a personal paper; the topic was also discussed by the Labour Party, the TUC, staff associations and several individuals. The general, but not unanimous, weight of opinion was in favour of a change, either to a Public Service Commission or to a new department.

Relations with Ministers were not widely discussed, but were dealt with by the Labour Party and some individuals. The Labour Party was also in favour of a Ministerial 'cabinet' on the French model. Some papers suggested a looser system of *ad hoc* personal appointments; this received fullest treatment in the paper by the Fabian Society, but it was also discussed by, among others, the Liberal Party, the TUC, and the IPCS. A number of papers commented on the convention that civil servants should be anonymous, most thought it should be relaxed.

The Fulton Committee found it surprising that there was so much agreement in the vast amount of evidence presented. To some extent the main lines of its approach had been laid down in published writings before the Committee began work, and the evidence then submitted tended to originate from individuals and organisations concerned in various ways with reform movements, and from bodies whose interests might be affected by the recommendations of the Committee – for example, staff associations and institutions that worked closely with the official bureaucracy. Other evidence came from academics or thoughtful outsiders – many of whom had recently retired or resigned from the Service and felt that they had opinions that might interest the Committee, and some of whom also felt that they could at last freely express in public their views about the Service in which they had worked.

However, the main characteristic of all this evidence was that it did not analyse in depth but merely identified the problems from various viewpoints and suggested possible solutions. It was not concerned with rigorously analysing suggested solutions in relation to generally accepted problems; indeed, for at least some of the commissioned research this was specifically excluded from the terms of reference on the ground that that was what the Committee was for. And it could well be argued that the small amount of research that was actually commissioned would not have been necessary at all if the Treasury had been more proficient at performing its personnel management functions.

A SUMMARY OF THE REPORT[17]

General diagnosis

In Chapter 1 the Committee stated that the 'Home Civil Service today is still fundamentally the product of the nineteenth-century philosophy of the Northcote-Trevelyan Report. The tasks it faces are those of the second half of the twentieth century. This is what we have found; it is what we seek to remedy.' Because the reports of Northcote and Trevelyan on *The Organisation of the Permanent Civil Service* (1853) and Macaulay's *Report on the Indian Civil Service* (1854) had been so influential, the Fulton Committee reproduced the full text of both reports in an Appendix.

It was stated that as the Civil Service grew from the mid-nineteenth century there emerged the tradition of the 'all-rounder', or 'amateur', and the Committee added: 'the basic principles and philosophy of the Northcote-Trevelyan Report have prevailed: the essential features of their structure have remained'. However, the role of government had greatly changed and its new tasks amounted to a much more active and positive engagement in public affairs. In the view of the Committee the structure and practices of the Service had not kept up with the changing tasks and its defects could nearly all be attributed to this. Consequently, it was believed that the Service was in need of fundamental change to fit it for the most efficient discharge of contemporary and prospective responsibilities of government. The Committee therefore made proposals intended to create a fully professional and dynamic Service in which specialists would have more training in management and greater responsibilities, and administrators would be no longer gifted amateurs but instead would possess a greater degree of specialisation.

The guiding principle which the Committee recommended for the future development of the Service was 'look at the job first'. 'The Civil Service', it asserted, 'must continuously review the tasks it is called upon to perform and the possible ways in which it might perform them; it should then think out what new skills and kinds of men are needed, and how these men can be found, trained and deployed.' The Committee stated that the root of much of their criticism was that this principle had not been observed and the urgent need for fundamental reform had been obscured by such strengths of the Service as its capacity for improvisation, the exceptional ability, integrity and impartiality of men and women at all levels, and the strong sense of public service.

Lord Simey, in his reservation to Chapter 1, stated that in his opinion the chapter was unfair to the Civil Service, because it failed to recognise the great contributions the Service made during the two World Wars and the transition from war to peace, and gave a misleading impression of its future potential. He pointed out that the main contemporary characteristics of the Service were twentieth-century developments. Instead of something approaching revolutionary change, he believed that necessary reforms could be obtained by encouraging the evolution of the present situation, with amendments in direction and emphasis. Because the Civil Service would always need the best brains known to teachers in schools and universities, Simey did not accept that the 'generalist' was obsolete at all levels, and he therefore stated that the task for the future was not one of total reconstruction of an obsolete institution, but an appropriate use of its potentialities to provide a basis for future reforms.

The cult of the generalist
The cult of the 'generalist' (or philosophy of the 'amateur' or 'allrounder') refers to the often-held belief that the ideal administrator is a gifted layman who, moving frequently from job to job within the Service, can take a practical view of any problem, irrespective of subject matter, in the light of his knowledge and experience of the government machine. The Report stated that 'the cult is obsolete at all levels and in all parts of the Service'.

The Committee explained that the jobs of civil servants are immensely various and some of their work has no counterpart in business or, indeed, anywhere outside the government service; 'as a body, civil servants today have to be equipped to tackle the political, scientific, social, economic and technical problems of our time. . . . In short, the

Civil Service is no place for the amateur. It must be staffed by men and women who are truly professional.' 'Professionalism' in this context meant both being skilled in one's job and having a fundamental knowledge of and deep familiarity with a subject.

In the opinion of the Committee the Service needed to be quicker to recognise the contribution new professional skills could make to its work, for it had not always appreciated the need for new kinds of specialism quickly enough or recruited enough specialists of the high quality that the public interest demanded nor had it allowed the specialists to carry enough responsibility.

The Service needed also to develop more fully the professionalism of the 'generalists' who are members of the Administrative and Executive Classes. According to the Committee, they were often required to give advice on subjects they did not sufficiently understand or take decisions whose significance they did not grasp, and this could lead to bad policy-making and inefficient methods for implementing policies.

In future, it would not be enough for a 'generalist' civil servant to be expert in running the government machine, he would also have to acquire 'the basic concepts and knowledge whether social, economic, industrial or financial relevant to his area of administration and appropriate to his level of responsibility'. This meant that a 'generalist' must specialise in the subject matter of his work. For example, some civil servants were doing work that was primarily economic and financial, others work that was essentially social. The Committee recommended that in future the work should be distinguished into such types so that the civil servants could receive specially devised training courses in relevant subjects and have their careers planned accordingly.

The system of classes

When the Report was written there were forty-seven general service and similar classes whose members were distributed across the Service as a whole, and 1,400 departmental classes whose members worked in one department only. Each civil servant was recruited on entry to a particular class, depending on the kind of work he applied for and his qualifications for it, and each class had its own career structure and separate pay scale. The system of classes therefore divided the Service 'both horizontally (between higher and lower in the same broad area of work) and vertically (between different skills, professions or disciplines)'.

The Committee found that there was often no discernable difference in content between work done at the lower level of one class and the upper levels of the one beneath it. The system impeded the work of the

Service, hampered the Service in adapting itself to new tasks, prevented the best use of individual talent, contributed to the inequality of promotion prospects, caused frustration and resentment, and impeded the entry into wider management of those well fitted for it. The system of classes was too crude an instrument for the purpose of matching men to jobs and the word 'class' produced feelings of inferiority.

The Committee therefore recommended that classes as such should be abolished. Instead, all civil servants should be organised in a single grading structure in which there were an appropriate number of different pay-levels matching different levels of skill and responsibility. This proposal would merge not only the Administrative, Executive and Clerical Classes, but also the Scientific Officer, Experimental Officer and Scientific Assistant Classes, the Works Group of Professional Classes, the Technical Works, Engineering and Allied Classes and the Architectural and Engineering Draughtsman Classes. Equally, messengers, typists and machine operators would cease to belong to separate classes.

However, at all levels where the work required civil servants to specialise, 'occupational groups' would be needed. There would be a great variety of these, each engaged in a 'block of work . . . determined . . . by what is required for the most efficient achievement of its objectives', and civil servants would generally be recruited and trained as members of them. Such occupational groups would tend to develop their own career patterns and during the early years of a man's career the Committee would expect him to remain within the specialism or group for which he was trained. The Committee thought there would be about twenty grades from the bottom to the top in each occupational group.

Whilst this proposal did not, in the Committee's view, imply a departure from the principle established by the Priestley Royal Commission 1953–55, of 'fair comparison with the current remuneration of outside staffs employed on broadly comparable work', it did imply the application of job-evaluation techniques, though it thought the task might not be as massive as it might appear. Over wide areas of the Service jobs could be grouped into 'families' for grading purposes so that the numbers that had to be analysed in detail were only a proportion of the whole. This work of job evaluation was to be one of the tasks of the new Civil Service Department recommended by the Committee.

Opportunities for specialists
As far as specialists were concerned, the Committee considered that many scientists, engineers and members of other specialist classes were

not given the opportunity to exercise full authority for their work. This was partly because the policy and financial aspects of their work were reserved for a parallel group of 'generalist' administrators and partly because many specialists were equipped to practise only their own specialism.

Although the Committee recommended that administrators should receive more specialised training, the report stated that they should not replace those specialists (e.g. engineers, accountants, economists, sociologists) whose primary concern is the practice of their specialism. On the contrary, the Committee explained that the emphasis placed throughout the Report on the recommendation that the Service should develop greater professionalism, meant that the specialists should be given 'more training in management and greater responsibilities', whilst in each department the old concept of the gifted amateur would give way to one of greater specialisation and there would be a blend of administrators from various groups together with the various specialists.

The Committee felt also that the Civil Service should be so structured that all civil servants could make a full contribution to the work of government. This would be easier to achieve with the proposed new grading structure, for specialist staff would then be able more easily to contribute to policy-making and management. In the view of the Committee it was of fundamental importance to change the structure of the Service, for, it said, 'as long as a structure based on classes persists, the attitudes and practices associated with it will hinder the efforts of management to open up careers to all the talents'.

Civil servants as managers
Another of the defects in the Civil Service seen by the Committee was that too few civil servants were skilled managers. One reason for this was that most of their work was not managerial, and 'civil servants, particularly members of the Administrative Class, have to spend a great deal of their time preparing explanatory briefs, answers to Parliamentary Questions, and Ministers' cases'. Another reason was that civil servants had not been adequately trained in management, particularly personnel management, accounting and control.

To overcome this defect the Committee recommended that administrators should become more specialised, and more training in management should be given to scientists and other specialists. The Committee also recommended the application of the principles of 'accountable management' in the organisation of executive activities.

Accountable management means holding individuals and units responsible for performance measured as objectively as possible, it requires the identification of those parts of the organisation that form convenient groupings (or 'centres') to which costs can be precisely allocated as the responsibility of the man in charge. Such accountable units should be organised into separate 'commands' which would correspond to the 'budget centres' developed in industrial organisations.

To keep departmental organisation up to date the Committee made four further recommendations. First, the use of outside consultants and the central management services of the new Civil Service Department. Secondly, each department should contain a management services unit, staffed by men and women with high qualifications, to promote the use of the best management techniques. Thirdly, major long-term policy planning within each department should be allocated to a planning and research unit staffed by some of the most able, vigorous and suitably qualified young (not older than their mid-forties) civil servants. Fourthly, in most departments, in addition to the Permanent Secretary, there should be a Senior Policy Adviser to assist the Minister and he should be head of a planning unit, and in some of the big technical departments, the Committee said, 'there may well be a case for a further top post for direction of the technical work'.

The service and the community

The Committee found that there was not enough contact between the Service and the rest of the commnuity, and this was partly because most civil servants were expected to spend their entire working lives in the Service, and partly because the administrative process was surrounded by too much secrecy.

The Committee recommended that there should be greater openness in a number of respects. Parliament should develop a closer association with departments. The convention of anonymity should be modified so that 'professional administrators should be able to explain what they are doing in managing existing policies and implementing legislation'. The Committee welcomed the practice of ministers bringing in professional experts and advisers of their own.

The Committee also recommended greater mobility of staff into and out of the Service. It noted that in recent years there had been few compulsory retirements of permanent staff on grounds of misconduct and inefficiency and felt the proportion could have been higher. Post-entry training courses should be shared with staff from nationalised and private industry, and there should also be a greater flow of 'outsiders' coming in for varying periods of work in departments, and more civil servants going to take part in work outside. Late entry should be considerably expanded, there should be more short-term appointments for fixed periods and more temporary interchange of staff with industry and commerce, nationalised industry and local government. Finally, to encourage greater mobility, the Committee urged that pension arrangements should be less restrictive and more easily transferable.

Personnel management

According to the Fulton Committee, career planning in the Civil Service was mainly applied in the Administrative Class, and this was too small a section of the Service, it was not sufficiently purposive or properly conceived, and civil servants were moved too frequently between unrelated jobs, often with little regard to personal preference or aptitude. To overcome these defects the Committee made recommendations for recruitment, training and the structure of management services.

The Committee found that in relation to recruitment, the Service suffered from the separateness and remoteness of the Civil Service Commission which ran the competitions, selected the candidates and allocated them to departments in accordance with the recruitment policy laid down by the Treasury. The trouble was that the Commission could not know enough about the needs of individual departments and was too little concerned with the training and management of individual careers.

The Committee therefore recommended that the Civil Service Commission and the work of the Pay and Management group of divisions of the Treasury should become part of a new Civil Service Department, and that some of the Commission's recruitment functions should be shared with the various employing departments – this would ensure that recruitment was directly related to the needs of individual departments.

The Report said that men and women who are not ' "specialists" should be recruited to do a specified range of jobs in a particular area of work' (such as the economic and financial, or social) and the relevance of the subject matter of their pre-service studies should be an important qualification for appointment. Those who are appointed without a relevant qualification should be required either to take a special training course at the new Civil Service College recommended by the Committee, or take a relevant post-graduate degree or course of study at the Service's expense, at a university or other appropriate institution. Thus, all new entrants, instead of being recruited as 'generalist' administrators and intelligent all-rounders, would be recruited for a specified range of jobs; the subject matter of a graduate new entrant's degree would be an important qualification; and in addition graduate entrants who were not specialists should be required to have a knowledge of numerical techniques.

A majority of the Committee recommended that in future non-specialist graduates, recruited by what was then known as the Method I competition (which a minority of the Committee wanted to see abolished), should be permitted to offer only papers with a direct relevance to the problems of modern government. The Method II competition would continue, though with an inquiry into methods of selection and possible ways of making the process of selection more objective.

The Committee recommended that men and women judged outstandingly able and well qualified on entry should be given a starting salary two or three increments above the basis for the entry grade, this was because of the concern of the Service to attract men and women of the highest calibre. Such people should be recruited into a training grade to create a fast promotion route and test them at different levels of responsibility and provide a sufficiently extended period of their training. However, all 'decisions which might shape a man's career should be based on post-entry performance rather than pre-entry promise'.

The Committee found that there was an impressive amount of detailed training organised by departments within the Civil Service, and it considered that departments should continue to run such training courses. But it found insufficient encouragement and reward in the Service for individual initiative and objectively measured performance. The Committee recommended that the 18–year-old entrants should be encouraged to take additional qualifications with the assistance of bursaries and paid leave, also that more civil servants should attend courses at universities and business schools.

The Committee recommended, in addition, the creation of a Civil Service College, under the general direction of the Civil Service Department, to provide specialist training for administrators, courses in administration for specialists, courses for top management, refresher courses and courses to help the best non-graduates compete with the graduate entrants, and a wide range of shorter courses in both general management and vocational subjects for all levels of staff. It would also be encouraged to conduct research into problems of administration and the machinery of government. A proportion of places on courses at the College should be set aside for men and women from industry and commerce, local government and the public corporations.

The Committee recognised that it would take a number of years to implement fully its far-reaching recommendations. However, it suggested that the most immediate priorities were to set up the Civil Service Department, designed and staffed to carry out the basic principles of the Committee's recommendations, and also to set up an extensive training programme so that serving civil servants who had not been given adequate opportunities for training in the past, could acquire the knowledge and skills they needed.

AFTER THE REPORT WAS PUBLISHED

The Report was published on 26 June 1968 and had a mixed reception. It was given a great deal of publicity on radio, television, and in the press but it is questionable whether the Report would have attracted so much attention if it had been less critical in its first chapter.

The initial reaction from the FDA was that 'a lot of the Committee's recommendations seem sensible', but the Report 'turns out to be very much like the curate's egg'.[18] Comment from the CSCA emphasised that 'the recommendations are general rather than specific. They demand close and comprehensive study.'[19] The IPCS issued a statement to the press on the day the Report was published saying that it welcomed the recommendations in principle, and pledging its whole-hearted support to implement the principles advocated by the Fulton Committee.[20] There was a general welcome for the proposal to reform the class structure, for increased provision for training, and for the aim of a new Civil Service Department to raise management standards. But on the other hand, the General Secretary of the Society of Civil Servants may be regarded as representative of staff association views when he wrote: 'What the Service is entitled to resent, however, is criticism based on sweeping generalisations which in many cases do not appear to be supported by positive evidence and which in other cases seem to reflect preoccupations about or misconceptions of Civil Service practice and procedures.'[21] The newspapers made similarly qualified comments of welcome. *The Times* said that 'the committee offers a lot of good advice . . . [but] its report is rather narrowly conceived. . . . The report is heavy in the technical appraisal of immediate practical problems, and light in political reflection. It is a thoroughly contemporary essay.'[22] One of the most forthright comments appeared in *The Economist*: 'Lord Fulton's committee has tended to catch the headlines with its flowery assault on "amateurism" in Whitehall, and pays only rather grudging tribute to British bureaucratic virtues . . . [the] first chapter is close to being rude, and . . . seems partly designed to make the popular newspapers say the Report is revolutionary; but . . . is then followed by proposals for reform which are themselves – although very worthwhile in parts, and concurring with current soft-centre conventional wisdom almost in whole – sometimes surprisingly unprofessional in their grasp of the arts of organisation and man-management.'[23]

On the day the Report was published the Prime Minister made an announcement in which he said that the Government accepted the proposal to establish a new Civil Service Department covering the previous responsibilities of the Pay and Management Divisions of the Treasury, and the Civil Service Commission. The new department was formally established from 1 November 1968; the Lord Privy Seal (Lord Shackleton) was appointed by the Prime Minister to assist him in the day-to-day operation of it and the Permanent Secretary became Head of the Home Civil Service. Because the CSD was established in this way, by Order in Council,[24] and the Prime Minister retained the ministerial responsibility he already had with no additional pay, the changes were not embodied in an Act of Parliament.

On 21 November 1968, during the debate on the Fulton Report, the Prime Minister announced in the House of Commons that the Government had rejected the majority recommendation of the Committee that the selection of graduate entrants to administrative work should be deliberately weighted in favour of those whose university studies had been subjects thought closely relevant to Civil Service work. This was further emphasised in the 1968 Annual Report of the Civil Service Commission which said: 'Our aim will be to continue to select the best people without regard to the subject of their first degree.'[25]

In the House of Commons debate the Prime Minister also announced the setting up of an inquiry under Mr J. G. W. Davies (formerly Secretary of the Cambridge University Appointments Board) into the Method II procedure for the administrative group of classes. The committee, which reported in September 1969,[26] found that the method of selection was 'something to which the public service can point with pride', for it found no evidence of bias in the procedures of selection or in the selectors themselves.

Another inquiry was commissioned from Cooper Brothers,[27] the firm of accountants and management consultants, into ways of speeding up central recruitment processes generally, while ensuring that they remain both thorough and fair to candidates. Cooper Brothers worked closely with the Organisation and Methods staff at the CSD and their report was presented in February 1969. By the end of that year the recommended changes (mainly the greater use of computers and restructuring the organisation of the Civil Service Commission) had been implemented and by the end of the next year the Secretary of the CSC reported that although the prime objective of the review was to speed recruitment processes it also produced valuable by-products in greater job satisfaction and appreciable staff changes.[28]

On the day of publication of the Fulton Report the Prime Minister also announced that a Civil Service College would be established. Later in the debate on the Report he announced that as the total amount of college training would be very great, three centres would be needed.

They have since been established at the (non-residential) Centre for Administrative Studies in London, plus two residential centres, at Sunningdale (in accommodation previously known as the Civil Defence College) and in Edinburgh. On 26 June 1969 it was announced that Professor Eugene Grebenik, Professor of Social Studies in the University of Leeds, had been appointed Principal of the Civil Service College and would take up his appointment in January 1970. The headquarters at Sunningdale was formally opened by Mr Edward Heath as one of his first engagements as Prime Minister, on 26 June 1970, and the Edinburgh Centre was opened in November 1970. The work of the Centre for Administrative Studies has been developed in several ways: for example, the course for Assistant Principals, previously lasting twenty weeks, has been extended to twenty-eight weeks with the additional time being spent on economic and social administration (two weeks) and five different varieties of six-week courses.

The Civil Service Department announced that central management training in the Service had been increased by nearly 80 per cent in the training year 1968–69, including twice as much training for all classes at Principal level, and that considerably more use was being made of external courses, for example at universities and business schools. During the Civil Service College's first training year about 8,000 civil servants attended courses at the College. In addition, by 1969–70 well over 200,000 civil servants were receiving formal training in their departments and in the same year 25,000 civil servants attended external training courses ranging from first-degree courses to short seminars of two or three days' duration.

It was recognised that before some of the more detailed Fulton proposals on personnel management could be implemented it was necessary to examine the work being performed by various groups of staff. Therefore a detailed questionnaire was sent to a sample of about 1,200 'administrators' between the grades of Higher Executive Officer and Assistant Secretary inclusive, 'designed to clarify and define the field in which they work, the kind of work they do within it and the kinds of knowledge and techniques that their jobs require'. In addition, reviews were made of personnel management practices in selected Departments to accumulate knowledge about the way the Departments concerned posted and trained their staff, the extent to which they developed specialisation and moved staff round, how far they aimed to take the wishes of individuals into account, their promotion and reporting methods and procedures, and the extent to which the heads of operating divisions and branches were regarded as an integral part of the personnel management and promotion functions of the Department.

In order to increase mobility of staff whilst at the same time maintaining the Civil Service as predominantly a career Service, a new scheme was introduced in June 1968 for two-way interchanges between the Civil Service and industry and commerce, mainly at Principal level, and the first interchanges under it were made at the beginning of 1969. More opportunities were also being provided for mature entrants into the Service: about one-third of the intake into the Principal grade in recent years have been late entrants.

As far as reforming the Civil Service class structure was concerned, the Prime Minister announced the Government's decision on the day of publication of the Fulton Report: consultations with Staff Associations began immediately to work out a unified grading structure. By August 1969 it was announced that progress had been made and it was hoped that an interim settlement on the problems posed by merging the Administrative, Executive and Clerical classes would be reached in 1970 and that the changes would come into effect in 1971. It was also announced that a scheme would be introduced to establish a unified grading structure for the top of the Civil Service down to the grade of Under Secretary. As for the gradings below Under Secretary, a research project was launched to see how this could be done through studying first how the work could be analysed and rationalised – about 1,800 civil servants were asked to complete questionnaires and were subsequently interviewed for that purpose.

On 1 January 1971, 200,000 members of the Administrative, Executive and Clerical Classes were merged into a single 'Administrative Group' within a new General Category. This was done by merging into single grades those grades in the Administrative and Executive Classes which previously ran in parallel (e.g. Assistant Secretary/ Principal Executive Officer), and introducing a new grade of Administration Trainee for graduates entering the Service from outside and also for staff of high potential from within the Service. In 1971 the Civil Service National Whitley Council announced that other possible mergers were being studied and hoped that there would be a merger of the Works Group and Associated Classes by 1 January 1972: this hope was in fact realised and on that date the Professional and Technology Category was formed. Other rationalisation has resulted in the formation of a Science Category.

On the question of openness and secrecy in the official bureaucracy, the Fulton Report had welcomed the trend towards wider and more open consultation before decisions are taken and the increasing provision of detailed information on which decisions are made. In June 1969 the Government issued a White Paper, *Information and the Public Interest*,[29] in which it agreed with the Fulton Committee in wishing to see more public explanation of administrative processes, a continuing trend towards more consultation before policy decisions are reached, and the increasing participation by civil servants in explaining the work of Government to the public. The White Paper set out the results of an examination of the whole subject undertaken by the Government, highlighted examples of what had been done to improve consultation and demonstrated the considerable increase in the amount of factual and explanatory information provided by the Government. It stated: 'Much progress has already been made and departments are adopting a more liberal attitude towards the release of information than in the past.'

The Civil Service has also started to develop the concept of accountable management as recommended in the Fulton Report. Shortly after the Report was published departments were asked to survey their work for areas where complete accountability might be achieved, and make proposals for implementation. An inter-departmental committee was set up to establish a programme for developing accountable management (to examine pilot schemes started in the Royal Naval Supply and Transport Service, the Home Office, and HMSO – the Ministry of Defence has also been considering the introduction of more accountable management in its industrial units), to examine the reports of surveys and proposals received from departments, and consider the problems involved in introducing accountable management in the Civil Service. In addition, the Civil Service Department examined the work of the U.S. Bureau of the Budget on measuring productivity in Federal Government organisations, and sent a member of the Department to study developments of this kind in the United States and Canada.

Progress has also been made on the question of early retirement or dismissal of civil servants on grounds of inefficiency. In February 1972[30] it was announced that Sir Harvey Druitt, the former Treasury Solicitor, had been appointed to chair a board with representatives from Whitehall and the Civil Service unions to hear appeals from civil servants who are to be dismissed or prematurely retired for reasons of 'limited efficiency'.

CONCLUSIONS

First impressions suggest that most of the Committee recommendations have been accepted: the major recommendations were immediately accepted by the Government – the Civil Service Department and Civil Service College were quickly established, considerable energy was injected into an extended training programme, and rapid progress was made towards restructuring the Service by replacing the system of classes with a unified structure. But the Report had concentrated on major points of diagnosis and recommendations (though some of its 158 recommendations are concerned with matters of detail as well as overall principles) and Lord Fulton explained in the House of Lords Debate that the Committee never regarded their Report as a blueprint and added: 'It will obviously need creative interpretation'.[31]

Some interpretation there has certainly been and in certain cases it might be regarded as almost amounting to negation. For example, in *Developments on Fulton*[32] it is stated: 'The Government's rejection of relevant academic studies as a qualification for entry does not mean, however, that they have rejected the more general Fulton recommendation that the Civil Service should select people with the *potential* for developing the kinds of quality and expertise which are relevant to Civil Service work; only that they have rejected formal academic relevance as an important factor in the recruitment of trainee administrators.' And in some respects the upheaval in restructuring to replace the class system may be more apparent than real: there may be no 'starring' as proposed by the Treasury, but instead new entrants (and others in the Service) will certainly be aware of the significance of who is placed in the fast stream as a Higher Executive Officer (A); and as was stated in *Developments During 1970*: 'For a large proportion of the members of the new Administration Group, therefore, there will initially be no apparent change in structure or nomenclature as a result of the merger.'

To some cynically-minded observers the net result may be the same as if the Treasury proposals had been implemented; or the whole Fulton exercise may not have been necessary at all if the Treasury Management Divisions had been doing their work properly. But this might reflect a superficial understanding of how policies on such matters are effected in the public service. In the first place, from the Treasury viewpoint, the Committee provided an opportunity to invest time at public expense to rethink solutions to management problems, and if the public service is as fully stretched as taxpayers tend to hope, there is rarely time for the luxury of such rethinking, however keen the individual officials may be. Secondly, this form of committee exercise, though in some respects wasteful of resources, is the way such problems tend to be tackled in the British form of liberal democracy. It enables individuals and interested bodies (including management and staff in the public service as well as the general public) to know what is going on and to present at length arguments for reforms they wish to see introduced – though in the last resort the decisions on which proposals shall be actually implemented still remain with the Government elected in the recognised manner.

It may be that it is the political role of such a committee that both affects the type of evidence (which tends to consist of a number of representatives of various interested bodies telling the Committee what it thinks the most serious problems are, and how they would like to see them solved), and the nature of commissioned research. Whilst it is true that the Fulton Committee was the first general enquiry into the Civil Service to commission research from outside the Service, the scope of that research and the time constraints under which it was carried out do not show the Committee's attitude towards research in a very favourable light. This is even more obvious when the research is compared, for example, with that done for the Glassco Commission which reported on the Canadian Civil Service in 1962. In Canada 176 specialists from industry, the universities and the professions were engaged in the research and approximately 21,000 days of work were recorded by the research staff, exclusive of the related clerical work.[33]

Peta Sherrif, in a most valuable article: 'Factors Affecting the Impact of the Fulton Report'[34] has suggested seven factors which may operate individually or in combination to affect the possible implementation of specific recommendations.

First, there is the degree of consensus among committee members: an important reservation from one or several members weakens a recommendation considerably (for example, in the Fulton recommendation for 'preference for relevance' in the selection of administrators, four members of the Committee disagreed and published their reasons for doing so in a footnote and the Government, in rejecting the recommendations at an early stage, made full use of the minority group's arguments). Secondly, there is the degree to which recommendations reflect widely held opinions about desirable change, though this may lay the Committee open to charges of being evolutionary rather than revolutionary (for example, the proposal for a Civil Service College: training is fashionable in the second half of the twentieth century, the Treasury Centre for Administrative Studies had already been set up in 1963, and a special committee on training – the Osmond Committee – had been set up and recommended additional emphasis on training). Thirdly, the degree of specificity of a recommendation is an important factor (for example, two of the 158 recommendations were that 'The Service should pay continuing attention to the problem of determining the right retiring age in the light of current research and national policies towards retirement' and 'The Service should continue to recruit staff for doing research work'; in such cases the Service can continue to do as it pleases without contradicting the recommendations, though implementing more specific recommendations might have greater impact on the Service). Fourthly, there is the extent of information available to the Committee on a particular topic, so that recommendations based on incomplete evidence must be hesitant: the research commissioned by the Committee was on a very small scale, and whilst 'what people think' is interesting evidence, in certain fields wide-ranging data, perhaps of a comparative kind, could have been more useful and strengthened the Committee's recommendations (Peta Sherrif draws attention to the Committee's recognition of ' . . . the need for greater mobility between the Service and the outside world, and the case for preserving pension rights on voluntary leaving . . .', and finds amusing the Committee's euphemism for the limited information: ' . . . there has been a great deal of evidence, no part of which however stands out as a full-scale treatment of the subject'). Fifthly, a recommendation's success may be influenced by the degree to which it is awkward (for example, the recommendation for early retirement of those members of the senior ranks of the Home Civil Service whose retirement is desirable 'in the public interest' because they have become exhausted in the public service, would be difficult to implement publicly in individual cases). Sixthly, it is possible for a committee to suggest a set of recommendations which, when taken together, are ambiguous (for example, the Committee favoured mobility between the Civil Service and outside employment but also favoured a career service). Seventhly, recommendations requiring tremendous super-ficial upheaval but which do not have revolutionary effects are bound to be successful – the publicity value is worth the trouble, especially where political decisions are concerned, for it indicates a tremendous willingness to reform (for example, telescoping forty-seven Service-wide classes and 1,400 departmental classes into a single grading structure may appear a mammoth task, but an administrative job may still be more likely to go to an administrator rather than a specialist, and Fulton's occupational groups may well replace classes in the post-Fulton Civil Service).

Many additional examples can be used to illustrate Peta Sherrif's analysis, but space does not permit them to be studied here. However, taken together they may well have a caucus-race effect as illustrated in *Alice in Wonderland*. With such a long list of recommendations, some general, some detailed, and some virtually contradicting others, it is not difficult for those who submitted evidence subsequently to reflect that they really did contribute to the recommendations in the Report and to the reforms implemented. And in a field as significant as reform in the public service of a liberal democracy that, in itself, is not an achieve-ment to be regarded lightly.

It seems obvious the Committee's work was throughout influenced by pressure from the Government: a report had to be produced as quickly as possible. This may have contributed to the lack of interest in research and to the willingness to spend so little time considering similar problems and solutions in foreign countries. It may also have encouraged the Committee to refrain from pressing for a revision of their terms of reference which did not include the machinery of government though the Committee found this a significant limitation on the scope of its work. There is little doubt that this pressure resulted in a less polished report than would otherwise have been produced. And the intemperate style of the first chapter may also have been the result of shortage of time, combined with an awareness of the type of sentiments that the Government would welcome.

Furthermore, the Fulton report appears a somewhat party-political document: this is reflected, for example, in the Committee membership. Although not a Royal Commission, it might have been expected that the recommendations would be the more willingly accepted in the Service because there were four leading civil servants on the Committee. The civil servants seem largely to have agreed with the recommendations in the Report, but, once on the Committee, there was little they could do between pressing their views in Committee discussions or resigning (which would have caused considerable controversy): for, by convention, civil servants on such committees do not write minority reports or memoranda of dissent. There was a Conservative MP on the Committee, but he was, of course, a very liberal conservative and known to be sympathetic to reform movements. So it is hardly surprising that such an active role was played by Norman Hunt, the Committee's only full-time member.

A significant number of the Report's major recommendations have been already implemented, though the way they have been implemented could mean less fundamental change than might at first sight be expected. A full and fair assessment of the Committee's work and consequences of its recommendations can hardly be made for some considerable time – when the products of new recruitment procedures reach senior positions in the Civil Service – and even then there will be uncertainty because so many other related factors will have changed. Some of the reforms, such as the implementation of Treasury recommendations, are likely to have occurred in time whether or not there was a committee of inquiry. In the final analysis the Fulton exercise may well appear, to a sceptical observer, as a political expedient for a government seeking to create a reformist image.

NOTES

1 Hugh Thomas (ed.), *The Establishment*, Anthony Blond, 1959. The essay by Balogh is also reprinted in Hugh Thomas (ed.), *Crisis in the Civil Service*, Anthony Blond, 1968.
2 Brian Chapman, *British Government Observed*, Allen & Unwin, 1963.
3 *The Administrators, the Reform of the Civil Service*, Fabian Tract 355, The Fabian Society, 1964.
4 See *Whitehall and Beyond, Jo Grimond, Enoch Powell and Harold Wilson: Three Conversations with Norman Hunt, with a Comment by Lord Bridges*, BBC, 1964.
5 *Let's Go with Labour for the New Britain*, The Labour Party, 1964. See especially pp. 7 and 23.
6 *Sixth Report from the Estimates Committee Together with the Minutes of the Evidence Taken before Sub-Committee E, Session 1964–65*, HC 308, HMSO, 1965.
7 *House of Commons Debates*, Vol. 724, Cols 209–214 (8 February 1966).
8 Desmond Keeling, 'The Development of Central Training in the Civil Service 1963–70', *Public Administration*, Vol. 49 (1971), pp. 51–71.
9 *The Economist*, 12 February 1966.
10 *Red Tape*, Vol. 55, No. 6 (March 1966).
11 T. 162/259.
12 D. N. Chester, 'The Report of the Fulton Committee on the Civil Service', *Public Administration* (Australia), Vol. 27 (1968), p. 297.
13 Boswell's *Life of Johnson* (L. F. Powell's revision of G. B. Hill's edition), Oxford, 1934, Vol. 1, p. 463.
14 The estimated cost of preparing and publishing the Fulton Report (as stated in the Report) was £51,854 of which £6,854 represented the estimated cost of printing and publication. The cost of the research alone is unlikely to have been more than a fraction of the difference between these two sums.
15 *The Listener*, 25 July 1968.
16 For a more detailed summary of the evidence, see Appendix K of the Report (Vol. 1).
17 This section draws heavily on my article 'The Fulton Report: A Summary' *Public Administration*, Vol. 46 (1968) pp. 443–451.
18 *FDA Monthly News*, Vol. 20, June 1968, p. 8.
19 *Red Tape*, Vol. 58, October 1968, p. 5.
20 *IPCS Bulletin*, July 1948 p. 26.
21 *Civil Service Opinion*, Vol. 46, July 1968, p. 195.
22 *The Times*, 27 June 1968.
23 *The Economist*, 29 June 1968.
24. The Minister for the Civil Service Order No. 1656 (1968).
25. Civil Service Commission, *Annual Report 1968*, HMSO, 1969, p. 10.
26 *The Method II System of Selection (for the Administrative Class of the Home Civil Service), Report of the Committee of Inquiry 1969*, Cmnd 4156, HMSO 1969.
27 See *Developments on Fulton*, Civil Service National Whitley Council, 1969, and *First Report of the Civil Service Department*, HMSO, 1970.
28. J. C. Seddon, 'Restructuring of the Civil Service Commission', *O and M Bulletin*, November 1970, p. 21.
29 Cmnd 4089.

30 See *The Times*, 29 February 1972.
31 *House of Lords Debates*, 24 July 1968, Vol. 295, Col. 1166.
32 *Developments on Fulton*, Civil Service National Whitley Council, 1969.
33 *Royal Commission on Government Organisation*, 5 vols, (Ottawa, Queen's Printer, 1962). See also G. V. Tunnock, 'The Glassco Commission: Did It Cost More Than It Was Worth?', *Canadian Public Administration*, Vol. 7 (1964), pp. 389–397.
34 Peta Sherrif, 'Factors Affecting the Impact of the Fulton Report', *International Review of Administrative Sciences*, Vol. 3 (1970), pp. 215–226.

3 The Donovan Royal Commission on Trade Unions

ROBERT KILROY-SILK

Set up in April 1965, and reporting in June 1968, the Donovan Commission was born of a period of acute discontent with the practices of trade unions and the system of industrial relations. It was the culmination of a growing chorus of demands for the reform of trade union structure and organisation, the system of industrial relations and for the law to play a more interventionist role in regulating the relationship between trade unions and their members, trade unions and employers, and industry and the state. None of this needs documenting. A glance at the titles of some of the books on trade unions and industrial relations published in the early 1960s is evidence enough of a fairly widespread dissatisfaction both with trade unions and the system of industrial relations.[1]

That the reform of the trade unions and industrial relations should have become a political issue was perhaps inevitable, in spite of the once cherished assumption that industrial affairs are best left to the two sides of industry. The responsibility that post-war governments have assumed for the maintenance of full employment, and its connection with economic growth, the balance of payments and social and welfare policy inevitably meant that industrial efficiency, and with it the role of trade unions and industrial relations in promoting industrial efficiency, should come under closer scrutiny.

But more than anything else, Britain's recurrent economic crises were responsible for the increased interest that was shown in the reform of industrial relations. Industrial relations were alleged not only to be in chaos, to be responsible for industrial inefficiency and lost output and exports, but were also commonly regarded as one of the major causes of Britain's continuing inability to balance its external trading account. In particular, unofficial strikes were a constant cause for complaint and were blamed for our poor economic performance. Though most of the allegations concerning the economic consequences of unofficial strikes were emotional in nature and based upon the most impressionistic of evidence, it was nonetheless true that 95 per cent of all Britain's strikes were unofficial, they were increasing in number and they occurred in those industries – coal mining, docks, shipbuilding and motor manufacture – where they were alleged to be most disruptive of production, the economy, and the drive for a surplus on the balance of payments account.

Yet what brought the demands for a royal commission on trade unions and industrial relations to a head were certain court cases, notably Stratford v. Lindley and Rookes v. Barnard. The judgements in these cases upset the long-standing interpretation of the law as it affected the trade unions. And it was the Trades Union Congress that took the initiative for a change in the law that eventually led to the setting up of the Donovan Commission.

The TUC were advised by Sir Frank Soskice that as a result of the Rookes v. Barnard decision 'it was now impossible to make any threat of a strike without running the risk of incurring legal action'.[2] Hence the TUC sought an amendment to the Trades Disputes Act, 1906, especially as its Finance and General Purposes Committee had come 'to the conclusion that the judgement could limit severely the work of trade union officials and the procedures of collective bargaining with serious industrial consequences'.[3] Thus members of the Committee met the Minister of Labour, J. B. Godber, on 11 June 1964 to seek a change in the law. All that they received from the Minister was the reiteration of the statement he had made in the House of Commons on 19 March, when he said that the Government thought that the law as it affected trade unions ought to be reviewed and that the Government would set up a committee for the purpose after the general election.[4] Throughout meetings and correspondence with the TUC during the summer, the Minister insisted that an examination of Rookes v. Barnard could 'appropriately be made only within the framework of the general inquiry into trade union law'.[5] And whilst the TUC wanted the matter of the Rookes v. Barnard judgement settled on its own, they nevertheless admitted at a meeting with the Minister on 20 July that: 'there was a strong case for a general inquiry but this would take a long time and could not therefore be the excuse for the Government's refusal to deal straightaway with the Rookes v. Barnard situation.'[6]

When speaking at the Trades Union Congress in September 1964 Harold Wilson, then Leader of the Opposition, referred to the Rookes v. Barnard decision and said: 'We shall legislate to put this matter of legal interpretation beyond all doubt . . . briefly and crisply without raising any broader issues of human rights or public policy.' And he went on to say: 'I see no need so far as this problem is concerned and as a condition of its solution for a Royal Commission into this question, which will take minutes and waste years.'[7] However, when the TUC leaders met the new Government's Minister of Labour on 29 October, the Minister said that the Government would redress the Rookes *v.* Barnard judgement, but he also obtained the agreement in principle of the TUC for a broad inquiry into trade unions and society.[8] Of course, Wilson in his speech at the 1964 TUC had been sufficiently ambiguous to keep, as the saying goes 'his options open'. Immediately after the last sentence of his (quoted above) he went on to say that: 'The practical problems which do arise in individual industries will not wait for years. They are urgent, and we shall deal with them by consultation and direct dealing between government and industry . . . whether a long-term look at the wider problems of modern unionism in the setting of modern society is desirable or whether they can be better dealt with by direct confrontation between our Minister of Labour and the TUC, this is a matter a Labour government will discuss with those concerned.'[9]

In fact, the Government appeared to have decided upon the Royal Commission themselves and obtained the acquiescence of the TUC by making a reversal of the Rookes *v.* Barnard judgement conditional upon their acceptance of the Royal Commission.[10] The discussions 'with those concerned' amounted to the Minister of Labour sending to the General Secretary of the TUC the draft terms of reference for the proposed inquiry. The General Council of the TUC made certain but unspecified 'observations' and 'suggestions' to the Minister, who accommodated them in his revision of the terms of reference.[11]

There can be little doubt that the Rookes *v.* Barnard case was a godsend for the Labour Government. The demand for an investigation into trade unions and industrial relations was almost irresistible. It was not a subject, however, that a Labour Government could deal with in a rational manner for the subject of trade unions had strong party and political implications. What the Rookes *v.* Barnard case provided was the excuse for the Commission, and the Commission provided the excuse for procrastination. The Government could claim to be doing something when, in fact, it was doing nothing. Or rather it had managed to pass what, to it, was a politically dangerous issue on to other shoulders.

TERMS OF REFERENCE AND COMPOSITION OF THE COMMISSION

The Prime Minister announced the setting up and terms of reference of the Royal Commission on 2 February 1965, in the context of remarks on 'the problems of the most efficient use of human resources'.[12] Its terms of reference were: 'to consider relations between managements and employees and the role of trade unions and employers' associations in promoting the interests of their members and in accelerating the social and economic advance of the nation, with particular reference to the Law affecting the activities of these bodies; and to report'.

Implied in the terms of reference was the assumption that the role of trade unions and employers' associations is to contribute to 'the social and economic advance of the nation'; that social and economic advance are complementary rather than often in practice incompatible; that there is a widely agreed definition of 'social and economic advance'; that economic growth is our prime social and political objective; that in some way the 'activities of these bodies' is detrimental to 'social and economic advance'; and that there needs to be greater legal regulation of the 'relations between management and employees' and 'trade unions and employers' associations'. The terms of reference indicate the overriding concern of the Government, and public opinion in general, with the rate of economic growth. Indeed, a 4 per cent rate of economic growth was the Labour government's panacea for all our social and economic ills. Though the terms of reference were vague, the Royal Commission's job was clear: How, they were asked, do trade unions and employers' associations retard economic growth and what can the law do to help?

These considerations, and the assumptions about the role of trade unions in society and the effect of strikes on the economy upon which the terms of reference were based, and the implications that flow from them, will be discussed in a later section. What the Government did was to appoint to membership of the Royal Commission people who could hardly be expected to deal with the problems in an adequate manner. First there were those, like Miss Green and Lord Tangley, whose knowledge of trade unionism was limited, to say the least. The former was headmistress of Kidbrooke Comprehensive school and the latter a director of numerous companies. Secondly, few of the members of the Royal Commission could be expected to either want or be competent to take a long-term view of the problem of trade unions in society. Only Andrew Shonfield attempted to do this, both in his oral questioning of witnesses and in his Note of Dissent. Finally, the government in appointing members to the Royal Commission seemed to be more concerned to effect a balance of affected interests than create a dispassionate and impartial team. Though it had told the TUC that 'members are appointed on the basis of their personal qualities and experience and not as representatives of a particular organisation'[13] it chose two names from a list of five submitted by the TUC and consulted with the Confederation of British Industry about employers' representatives.

The composition of the Royal Commission was, and remains, a source of criticism. It seemed to indicate that there would be either a compromise report of little value to anyone or a series of minority reports. It certainly did not augur well for the cool and disinterested report that many people wanted. It would, for example, have been inconceivable for a report recommending a greater legal regulation of trade unions to have been signed by George Woodcock. His membership of the Royal Commission could undoubtedly be defended on the grounds of knowledge of, and experience in, industrial relations – but it certainly meant that, so far as he could influence it, the report would be a defence of the *status quo*. The same applies, with only slight qualifications, to the trade union official, Lord Collison, and Professors Clegg and Khan Freund.

If the Government was genuinely interested in receiving a disinterested report rather than in passing what to them was a political hot potato into the hands of a mixed bunch of axe-grinders and pundits, then it would have been preferable to have commissioned an entirely different form of inquiry, perhaps a small departmental committee of experts.

THE EVIDENCE BEFORE THE COMMISSION

The Royal Commission drew up and dispatched a questionnaire to all trade unions and employers' associations and to individuals and organisations with special knowledge and experience in industrial relations. Some 430 organisations, persons or groups submitted written evidence, and a considerable proportion of these appeared before the Royal Commission for oral questioning. In addition, Dr W. E. J. McCarthy, a lecturer in industrial relations at Oxford University, was appointed the Commission's full-time research director. A number of research projects were undertaken and the results published. The Royal Commission sat for fifty-eight days for the purpose of taking oral evidence; members of the Royal Commission visited industrial establishments, attended meetings of national joint negotiating bodies, and made visits to Sweden and the Federal Republic of Germany in order to 'gain first-hand information about the system of industrial relations in those countries'.[14]

The evidence presented to the Royal Commission contained little that was new. Most of the organisations and individuals presenting evidence went through well-rehearsed and known positions. Broadly, those giving evidence fell into two main categories. First there were those we might call the 'hardliners'. They had many complaints to make of the trade unions and industrial relations and numerous proposals for reform. They sought a greater role for the law in industrial relations, greater control of trade unions and their members and for penalties to be imposed on workers for certain industrial actions. Secondly, and opposing the 'hardliners' were the 'soft-footed'. They defended, or perhaps rationalised is a more appropriate word, the existing system.

Naturally, it was those, like the CBI and the Engineering Employers' Federation who discerned major defects in the structure and organisation of the trade unions and the system of industrial relations, who made most of the running. The TUC and its affiliated organisations adopted a more defensive, even complacent, stance. Most of the written evidence of the TUC concentrated on a defence of the voluntary system of collective bargaining and the *status quo*, and contained little in the way of specific recommendations. It was as if they saw themselves on trial, but a trial occasioned by ignorance and prejudice. Once the 'facts' were made known the trade unions would be exonerated. It was just another Royal Commission, bothersome in that it meant they had to prepare and present evidence and participate in time-consuming activities, but presenting no real threat to their position. At least, their written and oral evidence gave no indication that they felt that the Royal Commission might produce a report detrimental to what they thought of as their interests. Indeed, the TUC adopted a high moral posture and presented their evidence as a contribution to the education of the more backward members of the Royal Commission.

There was hardly any common ground on which the 'hardliners' and the 'soft-footed' could meet. They did not share the same perspective, or frame of reference as it is now fashionably called, of either the purpose of industrial relations or the role of trade unions in industry and society. Nor did they agree on the 'problems' that were before the Royal Commission. To the former they were 'grave', to the latter mere anomalies that could be changed, if at all, by persuasion.

The starting point of the 'hardliners' was that the industrial relations system had broken down. In the words of the CBI, it: 'does not satisfactorily regulate earnings levels and is, in general, inflationary in its effect . . . the system pays insufficient regard to productivity and labour utilisation as factors in bargaining and, in consequence, makes little contribution to industrial efficiency . . . [and] the agreements themselves are not always honoured and that peace is obtained at the cost of broken agreements.'[15]

The EEF pointed to the same three major problems of inflation, inefficiency and unofficial strikes.[16]

More interesting was their notion of the role of trade unions. To the CBI, the EEF and the Inns of Court Conservative and Unionist Society, the trade unions were there to be a useful adjunct to management in ensuring that industry worked smoothly. And they helped industry (employers?) by ensuring that industrial relations were smooth and effective. As Sir Maurice Laing for the CBI said in oral evidence before the Commission:

> they should be responsible for focusing attention on collective bargaining and on industrial relations generally as to what is the right level of wages for the people in those industries; and . . . they should help us to settle disputes in industry between the trade unions and employers' associations; and . . . they should help us to develop our role in industry in the world so that our industry should be competitive and so that our industry can help to solve the economic problems of Britain.

and finally, as if an afterthought, he conceded that: 'they should provide a really strong representative voice for trade unionists and for workpeople, not only with us but with the Government and with the public as a whole.'[17]

The hardliners all agreed that for industrial relations to be reformed there needed to be more central control exercised by the trade unions over the activities of their members. Their evidence abounded with words like 'leadership', 'responsibility' and 'discipline'. What they wanted was that the unions would be put in a position where they would have the incentive and means to control and discipline their members. The CBI made this clear in its written evidence and argued that unions only supported unofficial action 'reluctantly'[18] while the EEF spoke of 'strengthening' the unions' hand in relation to its members.[19] 'Trade Union officials in general', the EEF asserted, 'desire to keep to agreements, they deprecate the strike in breach of agreement and will endeavour to get the men back to work.'[20]

The assumption behind this assertion and their recommendation for reform based on more central trade union control is that trade union officials decry unofficial and unconstitutional industrial action. This may well be their public posture but it is not, from the evidence produced by the Government Social Survey on workshop relations, their private view.[21] In addition there is the assumption that trade union leaders have what the Survey calls 'unused control capacity' and are capable of enforcing discipline. The evidence produced by the same Survey indicates, however, that officials rely upon stewards to carry out organisational and financial functions and maintain shop floor loyalty to the union. For these and other reasons trade union leadership is consent leadership; the influence that trade union officials have with the rank and file would be quickly lost if they were to attempt to impose tight discipline. It is, moreover, ironical that the trade unions should have been asked to do what managements had patently failed to achieve.

The TUC did not start as the CBI and EEF had done, by looking at the major problems of the industrial relations system. Indeed, one could be forgiven for believing that so far as the TUC was concerned, there were none. As the Transport and General Workers' Union said in their written evidence: 'We have a system of industrial relations and a record of industrial peace for which we have no need to apologise; trade unions, in two world wars and in their grim aftermath, have deserved well of the nation.'[22] What the TUC did in its written evidence was to present the case for trade unionism. Where it touched upon contemporary problems it gave its views *en passant*, as if it were all a tiresome business that really did not need discussing. The same attitude was also evident in their oral evidence. In reply to questions from the Royal Commissioners they asked questions and took particular exceptions to Andrew Shonfield's raising of principles and theorising. At one point Vic Feather sarcastically asked him if the hypothesis he was putting forward was an 'ordinary hypothesis or an actual one'? The attitude of the TUC delegation was epitomised by Sir Sidney Greene who, in answer to a question from Shonfield on the trade unions' immunity in tort asked: 'What is the object of people raising something which has not caused any difficulty?'[23] And went on to add: 'If you are going to run around clearing up all the cases where you think a problem might arise, then you are going to sit for a long time.'[24]

The same defensively aggressive tone permeated the TUC's written evidence. It contrasted the contract between employers and employees as not reflecting a position of equal strength, and asserted that the trade unions had been created by the workers to equalise their bargaining position and were, therefore, responsible to workers. 'That they are recognised in this country', the TUC said, 'is not due to the intellectual or moral force of the arguments advanced in their favour but to the efforts of working people in asserting them and exercising them.'[25] Trade unions were the means 'whereby men and women in employment can themselves decide how their interests can best be furthered'.[26] And as trade unions were the means that workpeople chose 'to advance and protect their interests', so also the methods they used must be 'left to the free choice of workpeople'.[27]

Turning to the more specific issues, on unofficial strikes the CBI and the EEF acknowledged that Britain lost fewer days than other countries. But the EEF went on to say that 'strikes in breach of agreement have caused much loss of production and disruption and, in the opinion of the Federation, are a major impediment to the economic advance of the nation'.[28] They submitted that finding the means of ensuring that

D

procedure agreements were observed was 'one of the major problems facing industry today'.[29] The CBI argued that, apart from the power which full employment gave to workers, unofficial strikes were also caused by the increase in local bargaining and the concentration of power in the hands of shop stewards, the failure of the unions to integrate stewards into trade union organisation and the inability of the unions to exercise control over them. It argued that the main remedies were 'to be sought on the trade union side – in improving communications and control within the unions, and in making it unprofitable for officials and members to disregard agreements'.[30]

Thus the CBI and the EEF suggested that there should be changes in the law of tort. Under the system as it then operated, trade unions and their members were immune from actions in tort. They could not, for example, be sued for conspiracy, for inducing a breach of contract or for intimidation. The CBI invited the Royal Commission to consider limiting this immunity. They suggested that immunity in tort should 'only apply to acts in furtherance of a trade dispute arising between members of the union concerned and their employers'.[31] A trade union and its members would thus become liable for damages caused as a result of strikes – official or unofficial – in breach of procedure, sympathetic strikes and inter-union disputes.

Furthermore, the CBI suggested that the limited immunity in tort should be restricted to registered trade unions. As a condition of registration the union would have to satisfy the Registrar that its rules provided for 'the control of the union's activities by the general body of its members and for the application of the principles of natural justice in relationship to membership and disciplinary actions'; 'the appointment of union officials and shop stewards'; that no benefits would be payable 'to members who took part in strikes or other industrial action which were not the result of union action in accordance with its rules'; that there would be detailed provision 'as to penalties and the classes of offence for which particular penalties may be imposed'; and no penalties for 'inadequately defined offences' or 'for failure to apply a restrictive practice'.[32]

The CBI further proposed that the Registrar should have certain 'continuing powers'. He would have power to 'enquire into cases where it is alleged that the rules have not been properly applied, e.g. in relation to elections, expulsions and other penalties'; 'power to require evidence as to the union's action in relation to an industrial dispute; power to instruct the union to take action, e.g. to encourage observance of agreements, discontinuance of unofficial strikes, withdrawal of overtime bans'; and power to impose penalties on unions and withdraw registration.[33]

The EEF expressed support for these proposals but suggested that it would be inappropriate for the Registrar to act as judge and jury. They suggested instead that the Registrar's power to impose penalties be vested in an independent tribunal.[34] Moreover, the EEF felt that the CBI's suggestion that penalties be imposed by the union on unofficial strikes might 'not be sufficient'. Instead it suggested that there should be 'clear provision' for workers taking strike action or such things as go-slows, overtime bans, the blacking of work before the disputes procedure had been exhausted 'be made liable to the imposition by an independent tribunal of monetary penalties'.[35] It suggested 'that it should be competent for a tribunal to impose a monetary penalty on a worker for every day on which he takes part in a strike or other action in breach of agreement. Furthermore such a tribunal should also have power to impose monetary penalties on unions if they do not take all reasonable steps to prevent or stop strikes in breach of agreement. The onus should be on the union to prove that they have taken all reasonable steps.'[36] The EEF wanted the tribunal to have flexibility in fixing the penalties and for penalties on workers to be enforced by deduction from wages.[37]

These two organisations also suggested as a separate recommendation what would essentially follow from an acceptance of their proposals outlined above. They both argued that the unions should be prepared to control and discipline those of their members engaging in what the EEF called 'acts of indiscipline'.[38]

The CBI tackled this issue under the heading of the structure of the trade unions and communications and control within unions. They pointed to the difficulty of reaching and enforcing agreements, of inter-union rivalries and demarcation disputes where there was a multiplicity of unions. What they wanted to see was a reorganisation of the trade unions on industrial lines. This, they believed, would avoid demarcation disputes, facilitate collective bargaining and make the integration of shop stewards into their unions easier. Yet in their view more important than changes in structure would be improvements in 'communications and control within unions'.[39] Hence they recommended the recruitment of more full-time officers; plant-based branches; the 'closer integration of shop stewards into union organisation'; 'more precise definition in union rule books of the respective functions of shop stewards and branch officials'; the 'regularisation of the position of shop stewards' committees *vis-à-vis* the unions'; the education of the rank and file in union rules and policy and greater training of shop stewards; and detailed procedure agreements covering the election, rights and duties of shop stewards.[40] And to show that they had left nothing out, the CBI argued that the unions would require more money if they were to perform the function the CBI would like to see them performing.

By far the most widely discussed and canvassed remedy for un-official strikes was that either collective agreements in general or procedure agreements in particular should be made into legally binding contracts. Traditionally, collective agreements in Britain are intended, as Kahn Freund puts it, to be 'binding in honour' only.[41] In part this is a result of the Trade Union Act 1871, which precludes agreements between one trade union and another being 'directly' enforceable at law. In the eyes of the law, an employers' association is a trade union. There was nothing in the law, however, to prevent trade unions and individual employers from giving their collective agreements the status of legal contracts. That they have not generally done so is due to their shared antipathy to the intervention of the law in industrial relations.

The Conservative party had long advocated, as had certain academics,[42] that collective agreements should be legally binding contracts.[43] In its evidence to the Royal Commission the Inns of Court Conservative and Unionist Society said that it recognised that many aspects of industrial relations can never become the subject of precise and legally enforceable definitions, and that there would always be a wide field over which the parties concerned would prefer to come to an 'understanding'.[44] Nevertheless, the Society thought: '. . . it would be advantageous if new legislation should make future collective agreements or any parts of them (but only so far as the parties desired) legally binding and en-forceable by law and against both the signatories and against their present and future members to whom the agreement related.'[45]

Although it anticipated 'considerable caution' on both sides of industry about entering into such contracts, it believed their advantages would lead to their increasing use. Those who were a party to such an agreement would be liable for damages for any breach of its terms, and the Society believed that this would be a 'powerful basis for securing the observance of collective agreements'.[46]

Both the major employers' associations examined this potential remedy for unofficial and unconstitutional industrial action, but neither was convinced of its efficiency or appropriateness in the British system of industrial relations. In its evidence the CBI noted that many employers were attracted by the idea but said that the Confederation foresaw many difficulties arising from such an innovation. It felt that unions would be reluctant to accept as a legal liability certain under-takings which they now gave 'voluntarily and honoured in the main', and they anticipated that such legislation would be followed by a host of other legal provisions, resulting in frequent references to the courts. Legal remedies would not, in any case, provide what the employer wanted most '. . . a good day's work willingly performed'.[47] The EEF pointed to several other difficulties which it believed would follow from the introduction of legally enforceable collective agreements. Not only would cases be long and difficult to prove, but also since the initiative for instigating proceedings would lie with the employers, this would tend to exacerbate industrial relations rather than improve them.[48]

On the issue of strikes, so important to the employers' associations, the TUC made the valid point that good industrial relations was not synonymous with industrial peace. It might well be that the absence of overt conflict disguised management or even union malpractices. They pointed out that working days lost as a result of strikes were lower in Britain than in most other countries and that the hours lost were less than those lost as a result of sickness and injury. More important, rather than treat strikes as a whole, they analysed them by cause and went on to look, albeit in a perfunctory fashion, at potential remedies. Not perhaps unnaturally, they concluded that many strikes were caused by faulty and ineffective management. As the National and Local Government Officers Association put it, unconstitutional strikes were 'usually a sign of ineffective managements and ineffective procedure agreements rather than of ineffective trade unionism'.[49]

The TUC isolated three main causes of strikes. Most were over wages but a significant proportion were caused by dismissals, particularly of shop stewards. To overcome this they recommended that the refusal of an employer to accept in employment members of trade unions, or the dismissal of an employee for trade union activity, be made illegal.[50] The third major category of strikes were caused by the refusal of the employer to recognise trade unions. To counter this the TUC advocated the reintroduction of arbitration at the request of one party.[51]

The TUC also pointed out that procedure agreements were 'often narrow in scope and one-sided in operation'. They were narrow in that many important matters were excluded from their scope, and one-sided in that if the workers had a grievance, they had to endure it until the procedure had been exhausted whereas management often made changes that gave rise to complaints but kept the changes in force until the complaint has been dealt with. Furthermore, they pointed out that if there were widespread breaches of a disputes procedure, it may be that the procedure was no longer suitable to changed circumstances. 'To order and require the parties to conform to the procedure in such circumstances' the TUC said: 'would be misguided in principle, quite apart from being impossible to enforce. It cannot be the object of industrial relations to achieve conformity without regard to the underlying causes of conflict'.[52]

As to the suggestions put forward by the CBI and the EEF for enforceable agreements, the TUC were 'firmly opposed to any proposal . . . to make collective agreements of whatever kind enforceable at law'. In their view it would have a 'serious and damaging effect on the generally enlightened approach to industrial relations which have been evolved in this country over the years' and was also a 'question of principle'.[53] The T&GWU took the same line and made it a matter of principle. 'We do not believe', they said, 'that legal sanctions against workers who withdraw their labour can be accepted in a democratic community in time of peace. The right of a man to withdraw his labour is an essential freedom which cannot, [sic] and ought not to be impaired.'[54]

The TUC had nothing to say on the other issues raised by the CBI and the EEF. In their oral evidence they were deliberately obstructive and simple. Typical of their attitude and their pragmatic approach was O'Hagan's answer to Shonfield's assertion that in some parts of British industry workers did not have a choice between two unions. 'Where?' O'Hagan asked aggressively, 'You name it, never mind generalisations.'[55] And time and again the TUC leaders turned the questions addressed to them back on their questioners, asking for examples, wanting specific problems, and refusing to be drawn into discussions of principles.

It was left to NALGO, perhaps one of the least militant of the unions, to reply to the employers' association's proposal for a more limited immunity for trade unions in tort. To them it was 'wrong and harmful in principle', would be likely to be more disruptive and ensure that more strikes became official.[56] As for the proposed more powerful Registrar, NALGO 'emphatically' rejected what it called 'far-reaching proposals for supervision of the day-to-day running of unions which are implied in the sweeping powers which it is proposed to give the Registrar . . . or to a special Industrial Tribunal'.[57] It objected because the proposals implied that there existed a simple definition of 'rights' and 'just' and a 'peaceful solution'. A 'more fundamental' objection was that it 'would also undermine the voluntary basis of our industrial relations system'.[58]

The employers' associations pointed out in their evidence the shortage of skilled manpower and submitted evidence on what the EEF called 'obstacles to the most effective and efficient use of labour.' Both the CBI and the EEF listed some of the restrictive practices such as overmanning, demarcation rules, systematic time-wasting to hold down bonus earnings or maintain overtime earnings, 'ceilings' on earnings, resistance to technical innovation, resistance to work-study, restrictions on the recruitment of apprentices or trainees, resistance to overtime or shift-work, and resistance to merit being the main criterion for promotion.[59] In fact the Government Social Survey found that only 14 per cent of managers attributed inefficiency to the trade unions. Nevertheless, in the opinion of the CBI, restrictive practices had 'seriously retarded economic growth in the past . . . and represent perhaps the greatest obstacle to future growth'.[60] And yet in spite of this wide-sweeping assertion, it dealt with this issue in a very superficial manner and produced little in the way of evidence.

As a means of eliminating restrictive labour practices, they said little, of course, about management equivalents, the CBI looked towards the development of productivity bargaining. It did not, however, believe that this could best be done on a plant basis. Plant bargaining, it argued, paid little attention to rates of economic growth, made planning with regard to incomes impossible, was inflationary, encouraged instability in the labour market through bidding-up, increased the scope for unofficial action, weakened the organisations of trade unions and employers' associations, and the inflationary features of the bargain spread more easily than their benefits. Moreover, the buying off of restrictive practices by productivity bargaining may encourage the development of new restrictive practices to be bought off. Finally, plant bargains would enable strong unions to obtain inflationary settlements from one employer after another. Instead they advocated, like the TUC (agreement on a vested interest here?) that plant productivity bargains should be closely related to the national collective bargain for the industry. And, like the TUC, they were vague as to how this could be achieved.

In addition to productivity bargaining the CBI wanted the development of the application of sociological research to find the reasons for restrictive practices and resistance to technological change, and to find out what makes workers happy in their jobs. This would be complemented by the education of workers in the relationship between earnings and productivity, the revival of joint-consultative committees and improved communications between management and workers.

As in other areas, the EEF was more positive and extreme in their proposals. Though they asserted that they hoped informal discussions would be successful in decreasing restrictive practices, and that what was most essential was a change of outlook on the part of the trade unions to the use of labour, they nevertheless argued that if these were not successful the restrictive practices should be publicly examined by an independent tribunal. The tribunal should have power to 'issue an order requiring those insisting on or supporting restrictive practices to desist therefrom'. A breach of the order would be subject to penalties.[61] Neither of the employers' associations seemed to realize, or if they did, they did not accept, that as Allan Flanders has argued, the responsibility for changing restrictive practices rests with management.[62]

For their part, the TUC pointed out that trade union means of achieving their objectives were various and could not be expected to be understood by those with a different perspective. They did, however, point out – in mitigation as it were – that uncertainty about employment and income was not an acceptable condition for change and argued that management had an interest in involving employees in the day-to-day decisions of the company as a way of obtaining their more ready acceptance of the part of the employees in the proposed changes.[63] Linked to this was the most positive recommendation the TUC had to put before the Commission. They advocated the participation of workers in management.

While the TUC were on the defensive on this issue, the T&GWU went on the offensive. It argued that action by trade unions to increase wages stimulated the efficient use of manpower. Again; 'practices which restrict the use of labour do not necessarily hinder economic development. For instance, trade unions' actions which restrict excessive overtime or excessive speeds may prevent faulty work or accidents.'[64]

And, finally, restrictive practices were based on social considerations for the 'common good' of the workers if not the nation also.

In the context of the Labour Government's incomes policy and related to the terms of reference of the Commission on the 'social and economic advance of the nation' both the CBI and the EEF expressed concern about the inability of productivity to keep pace with earnings. They blamed this for inflation and lost exports, and bemoaned the fact that it did not take account of something they called the 'national interest'. Though much of the gap between productivity and earnings was attributed to labour shortage and the willingness of employers to bid-up for labour, there were also, they believed, certain features inherent in the industrial relations system that exacerbated the situation. The CBI pointed to the failure of industry-wide agreements to determine earnings, to the deficiencies in trade union structure and organisation that made it difficult for a central lead to be followed and implemented; to the inadequacies of employers' associations and the complexity and variety of pay structures.[65] Yet other than their proposals for more central control, neither the CBI nor the EEF could suggest a way out. The latter saw no reason why national wage increases could not be related to the estimated growth of productivity but admitted 'quite frankly' that the problem of wage drift had still to be solved and they had no specific proposals to put before the Commission.[66]

As a final all-embracing panacea, the CBI expressed support for more comprehensive, explicit and detailed industry-wide collective agreements. These would help, they said, to eliminate strikes, increase productivity bargaining and reduce the incidence of wage drift, and aid the implementation of incomes policy.[67]

The CBI and the EEF assumed that the present distribution of income and wealth is generally accepted, and that further increases in wages must be proportionate to increases in national income. The TUC, on the other hand, announced that within the trade union movement there was broad agreement 'for a new move towards redistributing income and wealth through taxation'.[68] They did not think it fair to call for self-discipline in wages unless capital was treated the same. They believed it to be even less fair if the starting point was all wrong, as they implied it was. The TUC also pointed out that economic growth was not an end in itself 'but a means to greater economic welfare' and mentioned some of the costs of economic growth.[69]

The T&GWU took much the same line. They argued that in trying to improve the conditions of their members' working lives by collective bargaining, the trade unions did not militate against the social and economic advance of the nation. In fact, 'effective trade union action makes a powerful contribution to that acceleration'.[70] Trade unions did this by achieving a 'measure of social equality', making managements aware of the value of manpower by means of collective bargaining, bringing democracy to the workplace, protecting workpeople by legal advocacy in cases of injury and in pressing for legislation to prevent accidents.[71]

The TUC also took exception to the allegation that trade union action was often detrimental to the interests of the consumers. Trade unionists were also consumers, and were well aware of the relationship between prices and incomes. They were, they said, more candid in recognising that their primary responsibility was to their members and they took exception to being lectured on the need to think of the national interest from those who used it to disguise their own self-interest.

Coming down to specifics, the TUC remarked that wages in Britain were not high in relation to other countries and there was great complexity of collective bargaining. They were not against productivity bargaining. It had to be put, as the CBI had said, in the wider context of industry-wide agreements and, as the CBI had omitted to say, in the context of the cost of living, profits, and wages in comparable occupations.

And so the case rested. There was no meeting ground for the two sides and there could be none. Their outlooks and their attitudes were entirely different. The employers saw major problems and looked to the trade unions for help. And to obtain that help they wanted the carrot and stick of the law. The trade unions, on the other hand, would admit of little that was wrong. They rested their case firmly on the continuation of the voluntary system of collective bargaining and even resisted legislative proposals that would have been to their advantage. If there were problems, then they were isolated and could be dealt with piecemeal (as they had wanted the Rookes *v.* Barnard judgement dealt with), and by persuasion and consent.

THE RESEARCH PAPERS

If there was little that was new in the evidence presented to the Commission by the interested parties, there was not much more in the research papers authorised by the Royal Commission on a variety of subjects, and carried out by the Commission's own staff, the Ministry of Labour, the Government Social Survey, and several academics. Most of the papers were, in fact written by Oxford academics. W. E. J. McCarthy was the Commission's Research Director. Besides writing the first paper, he contributed to several others, though these were usually summaries of existing papers or theses. Clegg acted as the Father, McCarthy as John the Baptist and the other researchers as their disciples.

The papers share a specific orientation to industrial relations and it is not surprising, given the known predilections of many of the authors of the papers: a commitment to the Labour movement and voluntarism; a preoccupation with causes and facts rather than theories or ideologies; and an acceptance, with qualification, of the need for an incomes policy. The authors constituted a small, inbred group sharing a similar frame of reference, what has been called the 'new Oxford group'.[72] Most of the authors of the papers were known to be against the introduction of the law into industrial relations and most of the papers argued against it. The authors were 'fact-grubbers'. What they provided was an impressive array of facts and little in the way of attempts to link cause and effect and generalise from them. They summarised each others' work and quoted each other with approval.

It would be interesting to know if anyone else was invited to do research for the Royal Commission, or whether it was deliberately limited to what appeared to be a closed shop. It would be interesting to know, for example, whether V. L. Allen, Lecturer in Economics at Leeds University, or B. C. Roberts, Professor of Industrial Relations at the London School of Economics, were asked. Both are as committed to trade unionism as McCarthy, but in different ways – both from McCarthy and from each other. A wider catchment area of researchers encompassing different standpoints might have been more valuable to the Commission and might even have contributed to a different report. As it is, the way in which the research for the Commission appears to have been parcelled out must question the whole purpose and validity of Royal Commissions.

Yet more important than those carping criticisms is the absence of research in crucial areas. The clamour from the press and politicians that led to the setting up of the Donovan Commission was motivated by a fear of the consequences of unofficial strikes. This, too, was the main item of the evidence of the CBI and the EEF, and was considered by the Royal Commission to be its most urgent problem. One would therefore have expected the Royal Commission to inquire into the alleged economic consequences of unofficial strikes, especially as the belief that they are 'serious' was behind the demands for legal sanctions to be imposed on unofficial strikers. Yet while the Royal Commission saw fit to authorise research on marginal subjects, like the extent of overtime working, no investigations were conducted on the relatively neglected subject of the economic consequence of strikes, official or unofficial.

Again, many of those who wanted the industrial relations system dramatically reformed urged a whole panoply of legal sanctions to be imposed on workers and employers. Yet no systematic research was undertaken on the effect that legislation has had on industrial relations in other countries. The case against legal intervention into industrial relations *might* have been strengthened by the results of such research; it was certainly weakened by its absence.

The corner-stone of the Royal Commission's report was the recommendation that there should be a move away from national, industry-wide agreement to comprehensive plant agreements. This was no doubt due, in part at least, to the fact that the research team seemed to accept, almost without question, that industry-wide bargaining was doomed. Indeed, the paper on productivity bargaining, written by the Commission's secretariat, argued that the best level for productivity bargaining was the plant or the company. But no research was conducted on the importance or effect of industry-wide bargaining.

More important was the total neglect of incomes policy, which was almost equally reflected in the Royal Commission's Report. There have been relatively few years since 1947 when trade unions and employers' associations have been allowed to negotiate without some pressure being exerted by the government. Nevertheless, so far as the research team appear to have been concerned, it was just a passing fancy. There was no attempt either to estimate the importance of incomes policy or its economic impact, let alone its future use and the implications for trade unions, employers' associations and the system of industrial relations.

Turning to the papers that were written, their value varied considerably. Most merely summarised existing knowledge relevant to the issues before the Royal Commission whilst a few, like Marsh and Staples' paper on the check-off system, presented the results of original research. They also, of course, varied in the importance of the subjects they treated. Whilst some could be said to have been fundamental to the deliberations of the Royal Commission and were, no doubt, influential in the writing of the final report, others were only of marginal significance. If they had a common theme (other than the need for reform) it was that governments and managements must come to terms with the growing practice of workshop negotiation as opposed to national collective bargaining. They stressed the importance of the socio-technical system of the plant as a determinant of workplace behaviour. If attitudes and behaviour are to be changed then the so-called 'structural determinants' must be changed first. On the whole, they argued against introducing legal sanctions into workplace relationships, though they coupled this with arguments for a third party representative of the 'national interest' to be actively intervening, albeit in an advisory capacity. In doing so they were probably instrumental in turning the Commission away from the trend of press and political opinion which favoured more legal intervention in industrial relations. The Royal Commission's desire to see workshop bargaining recognised, though formalised, and to see the establishment of an Industrial Relations Commission to oversee negotiations, can probably be attributed to the evidence presented in these research papers. Again, the Royal Commission's recommendation for an Industrial Relations Commission was no doubt influenced by Marsh and McCarthy's paper on disputes procedures which advocated the setting up of a Procedural Commission; and the recommendation for a limited form of arbitration is similar to a suggestion of McCarthy's in his paper on the Industrial Disputes Tribunal.

THE REPORT

When it was published the Report of the Royal Commission was, ironically, more of an indictment of management than a critique of the trade unions, though it made many suggestions for the reform of the latter. Paradoxically, it criticised management and employers' associations for failing to exercise control over workshop relations and collective bargaining, precisely the criticism the employers had directed at the unions.

The Report of the Commission started by asserting that Britain had two systems of industrial relations. There was the formal system embodied in official institutions and the informal system created by the actual behaviour of trade unions and employers' associations, managers, shop stewards, and workers. Although this analytic section of the Report generally has been acclaimed, what it said was not new – to students of industrial relations at least – and is probably true of any dynamic economy.[73] While the Royal Commission accepted the idea that an informal system of industrial relations was not a peculiarly British phenomenon, it did argue that it had special consequences in Britain because of the refusal of employers' associations and trade unions to acknowledge and come to terms with workshop negotiation, and because the 'informal' system was often in conflict with the 'formal' system of industry-wide collective bargaining.

The basis of the formal system is the industry-wide collective agreement negotiated by employers' associations and trade unions, or federations of unions. These agreements are supposed to regulate pay, hours, and conditions of work for the industry. Earnings data supplied by the Ministry of Labour showed, however, that there had been a decline in recent years in the extent to which they determined actual pay. The gap between what the industry-wide agreement laid down and what was received in pay was covered by negotiations at the level of the workplace on piecework or incentive payments, additions to the basic rate, and overtime earnings. This indicated a transfer of authority in collective bargaining from the level of the industry to that of the 'factory' or plant.

Besides the negotiation of substantive agreements, industry-wide bargains also included procedure agreements intended to conciliate or determine disputes arising out of the implementation of substantive agreements. The transfer of power to the workshop has subjected these procedures to strain, with the result that they have responded either by abandoning any notion of common standards and settling disputes on an *ad hoc* basis or by handling a diminishing number of disputes. Either way, the result has been a distortion of industry pay structures. Though lip service is still paid to the desirability and efficiency of industry-wide bargaining, it had, in the view of the Commission, become a façade.

This analysis was implicit in the evidence of the employers' associations referred to above. But whereas the employers' associations wanted the trend to be reversed by reassertion of control at the level of the industry, the report of the Royal Commission argued that this was both impossible and undesirable. It was impossible because the informal system of workshop negotiation was based on the 'reality' of a change in power in industrial relations. 'Reality cannot be forced to comply with pretences.' It was undesirable because any attempt to mould the facts to preconceived notions not only would lead to industrial disruption but would also fail, as it has failed in the past, to provide the kind of regulation which is required.

Nevertheless, the Royal Commission argued that workplace bargaining suffered from certain disadvantages. They accepted Allan Flanders' description of it in his evidence to the Royal Commission, as being 'largely informal, largely fragmented and largely autonomous'. It is informal because of the predominance of unwritten understandings, custom, and practice which applies equally to substantive and procedural matters. It is fragmented because it is conducted in such a way that different groups get different concessions at different times which leads to a distortion of differentials and a chaotic wage structure. It is autonomous because the control of trade unions and employers' associations had diminished.

The Royal Commission believed these characteristics of collective bargaining 'explained' Britain's pattern of strikes. As has been pointed out, most strikes were, and are, unofficial and unconstitutional. The overwhelming majority are over workplace issues rather than issues applicable to the industry. They arise from workshop and factory issues and are invariably settled within the workshop and the factory.

Part of the explanation for this decentralisation of collective bargaining is the prevalence of full employment in Britain in the post-war period. This has increased the power of the workgroup and encouraged bargaining at the workplace rather than at the level of the industry. But employers' associations, managers, and trade unions must also share some of the responsibility for what the Commission called the 'chaos' of the British system of industrial relations. They were all to blame for failing to adapt their institutions to these new developments and for failing to devise quick and efficient disputes procedures relevant to workplace bargaining. Employers' associations were criticised for allowing innovations in collective bargaining (such as arrangements for redundancies, sick pay, pension schemes, and dismissal procedures) to bypass them. Management was criticised for its lack of a comprehensive personnel policy, for allowing the bidding-up of wages within the workplace, and for tolerating the existence of custom and practice in dealing with shop stewards in preference to union officials. The trade unions were exonerated by the Royal Commission for responsibility for wage drift and the ineffectiveness of disputes procedures. Multiunionism had helped, however, to inflate the power of workgroups and shop stewards within the factory.

The major recommendation of the report (upon which all its other proposals for the reform of the British system of industrial relations are based) was that the negotiation of company and plant agreements replace the present system of industry-wide collective bargaining. This recommendation owed a great deal to the evidence of Allan Flanders and the Research Papers on Workshop Relations. It also, of course, fitted in with the general orientation of the so-called 'Oxford School' the best representative of which, Professor Clegg, was a member of the Royal Commission; he is alleged to have written the 'analytic' section of the Report.

As the 'reality' of workshop negotiations cannot be made to fit the 'façade' of industry-wide agreements, and as the 'central defect' of the British system of industrial relations is the 'disorder in factory and workshop relations and pay structures', the 'remedy must be to introduce greater order into factory and workshop relations'. What the Royal Commission wanted to see established was 'effective and orderly collective bargaining over such issues as the control of incentive schemes, the regulation of hours actually worked, the use of job evaluation, work practices and the linking of changes in pay to changes in performance, facilities for shop stewards and disciplinary rules and appeals'. Accordingly it recommended that the boards of companies should review industrial relations within their firms and in doing so should have the following objectives in mind:

1. To develop, together with trade unions representative of their employees, comprehensive and authoritative collective bargaining machinery to deal at company and/or factory level with the terms and conditions of employment which are settled at these levels.

2. To develop, together with trade unions representative of their employees, joint procedures for the rapid and equitable settlement of grievances in a manner consistent with the relevant collective agreements.

3. To conclude with unions representative of their employees agreements regulating the position of shop stewards in matters such as: facilities for holding elections; numbers and constituencies; recognition of credentials; facilities to consult and report back to their members; facilities to meet with other stewards; the responsibilities of the chief shop steward (if any); pay while functioning as steward in working hours; day release with pay for training.

4. To conclude agreements covering the handling of redundancy.

5. To adopt effective rules and procedures governing disciplinary matters, including dismissal, with provision for appeals.

6. To ensure regular joint discussion of measures to promote safety at work.

The Royal Commission recognised that these objectives could not be achieved by boards of directors and managements acting alone, but would need the co-operation of the trade unions. This would require the reform of the trade unions. The Royal Commission recommended that unions attempt to reduce multi-unionism by mergers (especially in the engineering and construction industries), and in multi-union companies co-operate in negotiating a common agreement. In addition, unions should develop, as the CBI suggested, constitutionally recognised committees at the level of the factory; base their branches on factories; increase the number of full-time trade union officials, and regularise the status and functions of the shop stewards. To provide the unions with money to finance their increased expenditure, the Commission recommended a doubling of the union subscriptions and an increasing use of the check-off system.

It does not seem to have occurred to the Donovan Commission that the result of their proposals for factory agreements might result in the development of more, not less, trade unions. This certainly would be the case if factory bargainers registered themselves as trade unions in order to retain immunity in tort.

Nevertheless, the company and factory agreements advocated by the Royal Commission were seen as a means towards greater industrial peace. They were also thought to be the means towards the solving of some of the other problems of industrial relations dealt with by the Commission. Evidence of productivity bargaining presented to the Commission convinced its members that factory agreements were fundamental to the improved use of manpower and put in management's hands an instrument which 'properly used, can contribute to much higher productivity'.

Yet, the Royal Commission seemed to be obsessed by the engineering industry and its problems. It had little to say on the nationalised industries where national bargains are also company bargains, little is said about white-collar workers – especially civil servants and professional associations – and nothing on the steady and important emergence of national negotiation in the relatively unorganised distribution and services trades. Here, if anywhere, national negotiation needs to be encouraged, not broken down.

The Royal Commission acknowledged that change in the direction it advocated was, in fact, taking place but asserted that the 'pace of change is by no means sufficient to meet the country's needs'. Though the report did not elucidate these 'needs', it did say that it was 'impossible to be confident that voluntary action alone will achieve what is required in time', though (again) no time scale was mentioned. The report recommended legislation to assist the change to negotiation of factory productivity agreements without at the same time destroying the 'British tradition of keeping industrial relations out of the Courts'.

As a first step, an Industrial Relations Act should be passed, laying an obligation on companies employing more than 5,000 employees to register their agreements with the Department of Employment and Productivity. The agreements should cover the six objectives listed above as being the objectives of factory agreements. A company without such an agreement, either because of trade union opposition or because it did not recognise trade unions, would be obliged to report the fact together with the reasons for its failure to negotiate an agreement. Failure to register would make the company liable to monetary penalties.

The Act should also establish an Industrial Relations Commission with a full-time chairman and part-time members with experience in industrial relations and its own administrative and research staff. Upon a reference from the Secretary of State for Employment and Productivity, the Commission would investigate and report upon 'cases and problems' arising out of the registration of agreements. The likely subjects would be instances where companies do not recognise trade unions, where unions have refused to negotiate an agreement, and where agreements fall short of the Commission's recommended objectives. It would also be the permanent body able to carry out inquiries (which are at present conducted by *ad hoc* bodies) into the general state of industrial relations in a company and plant. No penalties were proposed for failure to carry out the recommendations of the Commission. 'The intention of the Act is to promote the reform of industrial relations by establishing a system of registration which will enable society's expectations in the field of industrial relations to be brought home clearly and unambiguously to the boards of companies and to trade unions; and which will make sure that they are given adequate assistance in meeting those expectations.' These proposals cut the ground from under those who advocated the imposition of legal penalties on unofficial and unconstitutional strikes. Nevertheless, a considerable part of the report was devoted to a consideration of various suggested legal techniques for coping with work stoppages. It rejected the idea of a compulsory cooling-off period and compulsory strike ballots. Britain's problem, the report says, 'is the short spontaneous outburst, not the planned protracted industrial action of long duration which is the main problem, for example, in the U.S. and Canada'. Most unofficial strikes are already illegal because notice to strike is hardly ever given to the employer, although he often has a legal right to such notice by express agreement, by custom and practice, or through the operation of the Contracts of Employment Act of 1963. The Commission also rejected the suggestion

E

that collective agreements should become legally enforceable contracts, and that legal penalties should be imposed on unofficial strikers.

Reaction in Britain to the Report was mixed, to say the least. Alan Fox claimed it to be 'profound' and 'comprehensive'. 'It is', he wrote, 'no mere tinkering with the system; it proposes a major recasting that would put our industrial relations on a new basis for the rest of the century.'[74] Allan Flanders saw the report as a 'victory of realism over pretence, of knowledge over ignorance'.[75] The *Sunday Times*, on the other hand, under the headline 'Donovan Funks the Issue', thought it 'fanciful to speak of the report foreshadowing a reconstruction of British industrial relations'. In the eyes of the leader-writer of that newspaper, the Report displayed an undeviating attention to the small print of the *status quo* and lacked 'a certain philosophical depth in considering the economic position of trade unions in the modern era'.[76] The apparent unanimity of the Report did not mean that the long-standing debate on the reform of the British system of industrial relations was at an end. The almost immediate rush to print of many of the signatories of the Report, helping themselves to some public exoneration for its short-comings, was testimony to this,[77] as was the reaction of those who would have liked to see a different set of recommendations.[78]

After the publication of the Report, the Secretary of State for Employment and Productivity initiated consultations on the Report with the CBI and the TUC as a prelude to the publication of a White Paper setting out the Government's proposals; this was published in January 1969.[79] As part of these discussions, the CBI and the TUC issued a joint statement on those recommendations of the Report on which they were in agreement.[80] Both organisations considered the Report to have been at fault in giving the impression that collective bargaining at factory or company level was necessarily best for all industries, but both accepted the need for considerable improvements in the voluntary system of collective bargaining, 'particularly by way of a more rational approach to factory and workplace relations and pay structures'.[81] They accepted the fact that the initiative had to come from managers, employers' associations, and trade unions; and they asserted they would begin joint action to review the relationship between industry-wide and factory-level collective agreements, disputes pro-cedures, and methods of strengthening the negotiating capacities of managements and unions at factory and company level.

The two parties also gave their blessing to establishing a Commission on Industrial Relations (the Government preferred this title to the similar one suggested by the Royal Commission). Yet, while the Royal Commission had recommended that companies above a certain size be obliged, on pain of a fine, to register their collective agreements with the Department of Employment and Productivity, the CBI/TUC statement suggested that there should, instead, be a system of voluntary 'notification' by managements of large firms of the procedural aspects of their agreements.

Later the two bodies sent separate documents to the Minister dealing with those parts of the Report on which they disagreed.[82] These cover most of the issues raised by the Report – from dismissals and trade union recognition to trade union structure and industrial democracy – but it would be impossible to deal adequately with them here. The major concern expressed in the CBI document was over unofficial strikes, and its principal emphasis was a reiteration of the proposals, submitted in evidence to the Commission, outlined above. The CBI felt that the Commission took too 'optimistic a view of the benefits which would flow merely from a wider recourse to factory or company agreements, and have certainly underestimated the difficulties both of concluding satisfactory agreements *and of securing their observance*'. The TUC, on the other hand, welcomed the Donovan Commission's rejection of legal penalties being imposed on unofficial strikers but, unlike the CBI, rejected the majority recommendation that the protection of Section 3 of the Trades Disputes Act of 1906 and the relevant sections of the 1965 Trades Disputes Act should apply only to registered trade unions. Furthermore, the TUC argued that machinery to deal with individual complaints against unions should be established under TUC auspices.

The White Paper followed closely the Royal Commission's diagnosis of the weaknesses of the British system of collective bargaining but accepted the CBI/TUC criticism that there was room for debate about the applicability of factory agreements. Nevertheless, it asserted 'the best way forward will often be the negotiation of formal, comprehensive and authoritative company or factory agreements', on the lines laid down by the Royal Commission.[83] It conceded too that the Government had a part to play in forcing the pace of reform. Accordingly, the White Paper announced the Government's intention to present an Industrial Relations Bill before Parliament, though no date was mentioned.

Among other things, the Bill would give the CIR a statutory basis, require employers to register collective agreements with the Department of Employment and Productivity (subject to further consultations on their scope), establish the principle that no employer has the right to prevent or obstruct an employee from belonging to a trade union, introduce safeguards against unfair dismissal, and set up a new industrial board to hear complaints by individuals against their unions. In addition, trade unions will be required to register with a new Registrar of Trade Unions and Employers' Associations and to frame rules on admission, discipline, elections, strike ballots, the appointment and functions of shop stewards, and the settlement of interunion disputes.

Before the introduction of the Bill, the Government intended to establish the CIR by Royal Warrant. It intended the CIR to be an 'independent and candid critic' of all aspects of industrial relations, 'a disseminator of good practices and a focus for reform by example' on the lines recommended by the Royal Commission. For this reason it would not possess legal sanctions. Besides being responsible for the general oversight of industrial relations, the CIR would have the function of encouraging reforms in trade union structure and services. To aid it in this purpose, it would be empowered to give grants or loans to unions for assisting mergers, training officials and shop stewards, and development of research services.

The Government did not intend to make collective agreements legally enforceable against the wishes of the parties and found 'completely unacceptable' the suggestion that it should be responsible for initiating proceedings in the courts against those striking in breach of agreement. It did, however, intend to enable trade unions and employers' associations to make their agreements legally binding if they so wished. Like the TUC, it rejected the majority recommendation that the protection of Section 3 of the Trades Disputes Act of 1906 and the Trades Disputes Act of 1965 should be limited to registered trade unions in order to reduce the number of unofficial strikes. Instead, it proposed two other measures to deal with strikes.

The Industrial Relations Bill would have given the Secretary of State a discretionary reserve power to secure a 'conciliation pause' in unconstitutional strikes and in strikes where no joint discussion had taken place. The power was intended to be used only when normal conciliation methods had not taken place or had failed, and where the effect of the strike was 'likely to be serious'. In these circumstances the Secretary of State would have been empowered to issue an order requiring those involved to return to work and desist from industrial action for a period of twenty-eight days. At the same time, the employer would be required to return to the *status quo*. Failure of either side to abide by the order would make them liable to a fine, deducted in the workers' case from their wages when normal working was resumed. If no settlement were reached by the end of the 'conciliation pause', there would be no legal impediment to strike action. Where a major official strike is threatened, the Secretary of State would attempt to persuade the unions to hold a strike ballot. If they did not, and if the Secretary believed the strike to be a threat to the 'public interest' or the economy, and doubted the support of those likely to be involved, he would have the power to order the union to hold a ballot. Apart from giving approval to the form of the question to be put to the vote, the Secretary of State would not interfere in the ballot.

In fact, the Government found itself locked in combat with the trade unions over the proposed Industrial Relations Bill and, due to the opposition of its backbenchers, it was eventually withdrawn.[84] Ironically, the new Conservative Government has now passed an Industrial Relations Act based on its own policy document 'Fair Deal at Work', which bears little relation to the recommendations of the Donovan Report, and which was published just two months prior to the Report of the Royal Commission.

CONCLUSION

It is the contention of this essay that the Commission did not carry out its terms of reference and, therefore, failed to deal with what Shonfield calls the 'problem of accommodating bodies with the kind of concentrated power which is possessed by trade unions to the changing future needs of an advanced industrial society'. It is further argued that the Commission did not adequately perform its self-imposed task.

The main, and most urgent, problem the Commission believed it faced was that of finding means to deal with the growing volume of unofficial and unconstitutional strikes.[85] They were not, of course, alone in their opinion. Most of those who have participated in the debate on the reform of industrial relations and who presented evidence to the Commission were of the same opinion. In their evidence to the Commission, the Engineering Employers' Federation, for example, put strikes in breach of procedure as one of the 'three major industrial relations problems today'. Where the Report has been criticised it has generally been on the grounds that its proposals for dealing with unofficial strikes are inadequate.[86] The figures of industrial stoppages during the period 1964–66 produced for the Commission by the Ministry of Labour certainly underline this widely-felt concern. These showed that something like 95 per cent of all strikes were unofficial and that their numbers were steadily increasing.

The figures in themselves tell us little, other than that most strikes do not have official union backing, to begin with at least, and that they are increasing in number. They were interpreted, however, as an indication that there is something wrong with our industrial relations institutions. This may well be true, though it is a debatable point. It could well be argued that unofficial strikes are a sign of a healthy democracy, that the release of frustrations in this way is better than the potential consequences of stored resentments. However, the figures assume much greater significance when coupled with the widely-held belief that unofficial strikes have economic consequences which might well be serious. On this point there is little evidence but many assertions. The EEF, as we saw, claimed that strikes in breach of procedure have caused 'much loss of production', and stated that in the opinion of the Federation they 'are a major impediment to the economic advance of the nation'. In their oral evidence to the Commission the motor manufacturers attributed the difference between a 5 per cent increase in motor vehicle production capacity and a 6·7 per cent decline in production in the period 1964–65 largely to strikes.[87]

Given the figures of the Ministry of Labour and the existence of the widely-held belief as to the economic consequences of unofficial strikes, it is not perhaps surprising that the Commission should have focused its main attention on finding suitable remedies. What is surprising is the way in which it went about its business. Two questions would appear to be relevant here. First, do unofficial strikes have economic consequences, and if so, can they be described as serious? This is a question of fact and definition. Secondly, even if unofficial strikes do have economic consequences which can be defined as serious, what, if anything, can or should be done to prevent or prohibit unofficial strikes? This is a question of both fact and value. It is essentially a question of political choice which has important implications for society, the trade unions, and their members. It was necessary for the Commission to have an answer to the first question before it could attempt an answer to the second. The answer to the first does not, except perhaps in an authoritarian world, necessarily determine the answer to the second. These are important questions and questions which the Commission failed to ask and, hence, adequately consider.

Let us consider that part of the first question which deals with the economic consequences of unofficial strikes before we move on to the second, which involves a view of the role of trade unions and smaller unofficial groups in what Raymond Aron would call 'the industrial type of society'. Though 'economic consequences' is nearly always intended to convey permanently lost production, this is an assumption rather than an ascertained fact. As Turner, Clack and Roberts point out, few studies support this assumption and some indicate the reverse.[88] Nor is the notion of 'serious' ever made explicit, though it obviously carries overtones of damage to the economy, the balance of payments and thus the standard of living. Semantics apart, little evidence exists on the economic consequences of strikes. It would not then have been unreasonable to expect the Commission to authorise its own research. Though the Commission saw fit to sanction research on such marginal subjects as overtime working and trade union growth and recognition, no research was undertaken on the economic consequences of strikes.

Nevertheless, the authors of the Report felt competent enough to discuss and dispose of the issue in less than two pages. They concluded that they had 'no hesitation in saying that the prevalence of unofficial strikes, and their tendency (outside coalmining) to increase, have such serious economic implications that measures to deal with them are urgently necessary'.[89]

The 'evidence' produced in the Report to support this conclusion is flimsy to say the least and is based on two main grounds. The first argument advanced is that a tally of working days lost in strikes gives a misleading indication of their economic consequences. The Report points out that the figures do not include days lost at other establishments as a result of a strike and which may be substantial, 'as is borne out by the experience of motor manufacture'.[90] It is fortunate that the Report should mention the motor industry, because this has recently been the object of an exhaustive study, part of which included an assessment of the economic consequences of the industry's strikes.[91] The findings of this study are particularly important in that the industry has a high and rising strike-incidence. It is the industry often quoted as an example of where strikes are most disruptive because of its interrelated production process and because of the industry's value to the export drive. It is, in fact, a good test case.

Like the Report of the Royal Commission, the authors of the study of the British motor industry note that in terms of days actually lost in strikes, no very serious economic problem would appear to be involved. But whereas the report based its conclusion, in this respect, on the indirect effects of strikes on workers at other establishments, the authors of the study say that 'even making a fairly generous allowance for unreported stoppages, and for workers laid off on account of disputes at other establishments than their own . . . the average time "lost" works out at about two days a year for each worker employed by the car firms, or only a little over that figure if the "lost" is assumed to affect manual workers alone'.[92] They go on to say: 'Even the car firms, in fact, despite both their high strike-incidence and comparatively low accident rate, might well gain as much by a substantial reduction in industrial casualties as by one in industrial disputes.'[93] Contrary to the opinion of the Commission, the authors of this study do not believe an adequate calculation of 'working time lost' substantially underestimates the economic effect of strikes. Indeed, they think there is some reason to believe it, on average, an overstatement.[94] The reasons for this are important. The study shows that the production 'losses' quoted by the motor manufacturers are largely based on planned, or conceptual, targets which depend upon a number of assumptions being fulfilled if they are to be achieved. They depend upon assumptions about when new plant will be available, the number of shifts and the amount of overtime that will be worked, track speeds, and sales forecasts based on assumptions as to the demand for their product. When analysing the reasons for the failure of actual output to achieve current production schedules they found that short interruptions had no significant effect on output and that it was difficult to separate the effect of strikes from other hold-ups. A calculation of 'loss of working days' due to strikes is only meaningful therefore as an index of *delays* to production. What economic cost can be attributed to these delays depends upon whether the production 'lost' was actually saleable at the time and whether – and at what cost – delays can be made up. On the first point most of the 'lost' production in 1960–61 and 1965 was not wanted by the market so that a large part of the industry's strike incidence represents 'the industry's substitute for formally-agreed means of dealing with recurrent labour surplus!'[95] It also means, of course, that the industry saves on its wage bill when trade is quiet. On the second point the authors show that despite mechanisation and flow of production, the system is flexible enough to allow 'lost' production to be regained, especially by overtime working. It is perhaps small wonder that the authors of the study should take exception to the official terminology of 'loss of working days' as a measure of strikes. 'Unqualified use of the official terminology', they say, 'bolsters the belief that strikes generally have serious economic consequences.' They prefer instead the 'strictly neutral term' 'striker-days'.[96]

The second argument advanced by the Report of the Royal Commission in support of the conclusion that unofficial strikes have serious economic implications was psychological speculation as to the effect of unofficial strikes on management attitudes. The Report argued that it is 'necessary to take account of the effects on management of fear of the possibility of strikes even if they do not take place'.[97] Managements may make concessions in the face of threats to strike which might have more serious economic consequences than those to which a strike might have given rise, though it is 'impossible to measure such consequences statistically'.[98] It is the unpredictability of unofficial strikes which is so damaging. This leads to loss of management confidence in making plans and is therefore liable to have a crippling effect on the pace of innovation and technological change, which is found in its most acute form in the 'endemic' strike situation.

One of the Commission's own research papers showed the 'endemic' strike situation to be untypical.[99] Another of the Commission's research papers produced overwhelming evidence as to the satisfactory nature of workplace relations so far as the participants on both sides were concerned.[100] This nation-wide survey of workshop relations undertaken for the Commission by the Government Social Survey showed that most managers preferred to deal with shop stewards rather than union officials and regarded their stewards as reasonable and moderating influences. It concluded that 'even an increasing volume of disputes and grievances, plus the use of occasional unconstitutional action, does not seem to the participants, to be incompatible with mutual toleration and acceptance, and a judgement on the overall state of industrial relations which is regarded as generally satisfactory'.[101]

Nevertheless, the Commission preferred to work on the assumption that unofficial strikes had serious economic implications. They therefore looked for their causes and discussed potential remedies. Whilst choosing to ignore the study of the British motor industry as to the economic consequences of strikes, they relied heavily upon it for an assessment of their causes, though they also conducted inquiries of their own. Specifically, disputes are over wages, working arrangements, discipline, redundancy and the like; all workplace issues. More generally the causes are to be found in the growth of autonomous, informal and fragmental bargaining at the workplace, and the failure of the trade unions and employers' associations to adapt their institutions to this new development. From their inquiries the Commissioners felt safe enough to be able to say that the causes were not due to circumstances peculiar to the motor industry but to factors present in many industries. It is not necessary here to elaborate on the remedies proposed by the Commission. Suffice it to say that the conflict between the 'reality' of workshop bargaining and the 'façade' of industry-wide negotiations is to be resolved by the negotiation of plant or company agreements covering all the issues at present a cause of unofficial strikes, and supervised by an Industrial Relations Commission.

Except for the assumption that things work better when institutionalised and bound by formal rules and procedures, few are likely to question the appropriateness of this suggested tidying-up operation. What is to be questioned is the manner in which the Royal Commission disposed of other suggested remedies for unofficial strikes. The debate on the reform of industrial relations centred, and still does, on the efficiency of the law in preventing and controlling unofficial strikes. The most widely canvassed remedy was that the law should intervene to impose penalties, of one kind or another, on those taking part in unofficial action, as proposed, for example, by the CBI and the EEF.

It is not intended here to argue for legislation on the lines proposed by the CBI and the EEF. Their proposals rest upon a number of assumptions about society and the role of the trade unions which are well worth elucidating – but not here. What is argued here is that the Royal Commission should have given more consideration to these proposals than it chose to. It could, for example, have commissioned research on the results which similar legislation has had in Sweden, Western Germany, and the United States; even accepting the difficulty of making transplants. Certainly, the proposals outlined here were *discussed* in the Report, in some detail and thousands of words. But all the legislative techniques suggested as means of preventing unofficial strikes were dismissed, with the exception of the majority proposal that unofficial strikers should lose immunity in tort and the note of dissent of Lord Robens and Sir George Pollock, arguing that unofficial strikers should lose all their accrued entitlement to benefits. And, to have one's cake and eat it, neither of these proposals show any appreciation of Alan Fox's research paper on industrial sociology.

Though it said that the law should be based on a solid foundation of fact, what the Report engaged in is the logic chopping of a lawyer. The main case that was advanced against legislation was that the present disorder of collective bargaining makes it impracticable to impose penalties. It would be an attack on the symptoms rather than the disease. Bargaining is continuous and fragmented and it would not, therefore, be possible to identify either the parties or the agreements. Yet the whole purpose of the Report's other recommendations was to end this 'chaos' by the negotiation of factory agreements covering all the issues now a cause of disputes. It would not therefore appear to be unreasonable to suggest that the law could play a bigger part in changing the system than is reserved for it in the enactment of its proposed Industrial Relations Act; and ensuring that these factory agreements are kept, once negotiated. When analysing the causes of the present 'disorder', the Report says that it is not due to the failure of the trade unions to impose discipline. This may well be true, but it does not mean to say that trade union discipline backed, as in the CBI proposals, by the law would have failed, or will fail. Indeed, there is a strong case supported by an even stronger body of opinion to suggest that the law can play an important part in changing behaviour. Though on its own admission the problem of unofficial industrial action was urgent, what the Report advocated was that we wait a little longer before determining whether and how the law can be useful.

Though they asserted that they were not against legislation in principle, it is difficult to avoid the suspicion that the Commissioners and their advisers had set their faces firmly against the introduction of legal penalties to control unofficial action, unconsciously at least; or that to have proposed them would have meant minority reports from Clegg and Woodcock which they implied they wished to avoid.[102] This suspicion that they had already decided against legislation becomes stronger when one looks at the way in which research for the Commission was conducted. This is even more emphasised if the press accounts of Clegg having written most of the Report in a few months are true.

Having argued that the Royal Commission did not adequately perform its self-imposed task by failing to examine whether unofficial strikes had economic consequences and by failing adequately to examine suggested legal remedies, let us now turn to the more important criticism that it did not do the job its terms of reference set it. What the Commission did was to confine itself to a discussion of the efficiency of certain remedies for certain industrial relations problems. What it should have done was to consider whether or not the remedies were appropriate to our kind of society. Even if we accept that unofficial strikes, for instance, have serious economic consequences, this is not in itself a reason for outlawing them. They may, as Garfield Clack has shown, have benefits as well as costs.[103] Conflict may be instrumental in bringing about improved methods of production or, on the other hand, be an indication that such changes are being introduced. Certainly, loss of working time as a result of strikes is generally greater in rapidly developing economies and can be expected to increase with an accelerated pace of technological change. It would certainly be difficult to prove that the most strike-prone sectors of British industry were also the most inefficient. Irrespective of this, the question of penalties is one of political choice.

The question before the Commission then becomes: 'What type of society do we want and what place have trade unions and unofficial groups in that society?' Is it to be a society which allows freedom for groups to strike at the expense, perhaps, of the general standard of living, or a society that places its emphasis on material rewards and hence outlaws strikes? To put what is a very complicated question in crude and simple terms: do we choose, if indeed it is a choice, to be free or to grow rich? The Commission might have made a start by questioning the implication in its terms of reference that social and economic advance are complementary rather than often incompatible, depending, of course, on how the terms are defined. It might also have questioned the implication in its terms of reference that economic growth is our prime objective, instead of assuming this to be the case. And again, it might have considered the costs of economic growth and how these can be made compatible with so-called democratic values.

If, as a society, we choose economic growth as an overriding objective and if this requires the outlawing of unofficial strikes, and greater regulation of trade unions is entailed, for instance, in the Prices and Incomes Acts, then we are still left with the question of how the supposed rewards of a now quiescent labour force are to be distributed.

This opens up questions of incomes and public policy which should have been central to the Report, but which were relegated to the end of chapters, almost as if they were afterthoughts. Indeed, the naïveté of its approach to this question is summed up in the last sentence of the section: 'If the decisions companies and trade unions take accord with incomes policy, then incomes policy will work.'[104] Only Shonfield, in his note of reservation, comes near to a discussion of these issues, but this, unfortunately, is a statement of belief rather than an assessment of the implications and consequences.

Once again the Royal Commission can be faulted in its approach to research. What it received from those organisations which submitted 'evidence' on these issues was opinion which could have been obtained much more efficiently by means of a social survey. It might have got much further by commissioning research into social policy and inviting critical comment from a widely drawn sample of opinion. This is to say, of course, the Royal Commission should have interpreted its terms of reference as being much wider than it chose to. Given the importance of the issues involved, it is inconceivable that it should not have done so.

No-one would have expected the Royal Commission to come to definitive or authoritative conclusions. These are not possible given the nature of the problem. What could reasonably have been expected was that these issues and the alternative courses of action could have been discussed and made explicit. The Report starts promisingly enough in its introduction but the end of the introduction is the end of its talk on 'society today'.

Furthermore, it did not, as Graham Reid has pointed out, indicate what it believed 'the functions of the industrial relations system to be, and until one has established some clear idea of what the system is supposed to be doing, it would appear to be rather diffcult to say whether the system is operating satisfactorily, or whether it is in need of change'.[105] What it did, as J. R. Crossley has argued, was to present the phenomenon of workplace bargaining as a 'trend' which, in good historicist fashion, contains its 'own justification'.[106]

The Donovan Commission ventilated a lot of grievances, but they were all well known, it collected and systematised information, but little of it was not otherwise available. It did not provide a balanced and impartial assessment of the issues, in fact it ignored them and even if it had not, its composition and research teams precluded a 'balanced' Report. It did not, therefore, contribute to a rational decision-making – indeed the new law on industrial relations makes Donovan look ir-relevant. For a time it allowed the Labour Government to delay a decision on legislating on industrial relations reform, but, as the

Conservatives have shown, it did not prevent it. What it did do was to bring to the attention of a wider public some of the issues involved in industrial relations and gave official sanction, important in itself, to known facts.

The report is, therefore, disappointing. It is disappointing because it dodged the real issue of the role of trade unions and unofficial groups in a managed economy. This opportunity for educating the public in the realities of political choice will not come again for a long time. It is disappointing because it ruined its own case by an inadequate examination of the evidence and by a method of eliciting evidence that must engender distrust in the efficacy of Royal Commissions. The Report will be remembered, if at all, as a document on the state of the British system of industrial relations in 1968. It is, as George Woodcock is reported as saying, a good handbook on industrial relations.

NOTES

1 Eric Wigham, *What's Wrong with the Unions?*, Penguin, 1961; B. C. Roberts, (ed.), *Industrial Relations : Contemporary Problems and Perspectives*, Methuen, 1962; and Allan Flanders, *Industrial Relations: What is Wrong with the System?*, Faber, 1965.
2 *Trades Union Congress Report*, 1964, para. 423, p. 353.
3 Ibid., p. 354.
4 Ibid., para. 425, p. 355. Godber's statement in Hansard, 19 March 1964. Vol. 691, c. 1598.
5 *Trades Union Congress Report*, 1964, para. 426, p. 356.
6 Ibid., p. 357.
7 Ibid., p. 384.
8 Ibid., 1965, para. 399, p. 377.
9 Ibid., 1964, p. 384.
10 The Rookes *v.* Barnard judgement was duly reversed to the satisfaction of the TUC by the Trades Disputes Act, 1965.
11 *Trades Union Congress Report*, 1965. para. 401, p. 378.
12 Hansard, Vol. 705, c. 940.
13 *Trades Union Congress Report*, 1965. para. 401, p. 378.
14 *Report of the Royal Commission*, para. 14, p. 4.
15 *Evidence of the Confederation of British Industry*, para. 55, p. 15.
16 *Evidence of the Engineering Employers' Federation*, para. 12, p. 3.
17 *Minutes of Evidence*, No. 6, Q. 938, p. 221.
18 *Evidence of the Confederation of British Industry*, para. 185, p. 34.
19 *Evidence of the Engineering Employers' Federation*, para. 33, p. 6.
20 Ibid., para. 24, p. 5.
21 Royal Commission Research Paper, No. 10. *Shop Stewards and Workplace Relations*, HMSO 1968.
22 *Minutes of Evidence* of the Transport & General Workers' Union, No. 30, para. 4, p. 1160.
23 *Minutes of Evidence*, Q.9679, p. 2690.
24 Ibid., Q. 9680, p. 2690,.

25 *Evidence of the Trades Union Congress*, para. 87, p. 30.
26 Ibid., para. 84, p. 29.
27 Ibid., para. 90, p. 31.
28 *Evidence of the Engineering Employers' Federation*, para. 14, p. 3.
29 Ibid., para. 23, p. 4.
30 *Evidence of the Confederation of British Industry*, para. 62, p. 16.
31 Ibid., para. 179, p. 33.
32 Ibid., para. 180, p. 33.
33 Ibid., para. 181, p. 33.
34 *Evidence of the Engineering Employers' Federation*, par. 34, p. 6.
35 Ibid., para. 40, p. 6.
36 Ibid., para. 44, p. 7.
37 Ibid., para. 55, p. 8.
38 Ibid., para. 52, p. 7.
39 *Evidence of the Confederation of British Industry*, para. 167, p. 31.
40 Ibid., para. 168, p. 31.
41 Allan Flanders and H. A. Clegg, (eds.), *The System of Industrial Relations in Great Britain*, Blackwell, 1954, pp. 57-58.
42 Most notably B. C. Roberts, *Industrial Relations Contemporary Problems and Perspectives*, Methuen, 1962, Introduction.
43 See, for example, *Action Not Words*, Conservative and Unionist Central Office, March 1966.
44 Memorandum of Evidence of the Inns of Court Conservative and Unionist Society, p. 32.
45 Ibid., p. 33.
46 Ibid., p. 34.
47 Evidence of the CBI, para. 174, p. 32.
48 *Evidence of the Engineering Employers' Federation*, para. 38, p. 6.
49 Supplementary Written Evidence of NALGO, para. 22, p. 8.
50 *Evidence of the Trades Union Congress*, para. 310, p. 113.
51 Ibid., para. 309, p. 113.
52 Ibid., para. 322, p. 117.
53 Ibid., para. 341, p. 122.
54 Minutes of Evidence of the Transport & General Workers' Union, No. 30, para. 192, p. 1183.
55 Minutes of Evidence, No. 629, Q. 10298, p. 2730.
56 Supplementary Written Evidence of NALGO, para. 12, p. 6 and para. 21, p. 8.
57 Ibid., para. 29, p. 10.
58 Ibid., para. 31, p. 10.
59 *Evidence of the Confederation of British Industry*, para. 77, p. 18.
60 Ibid., para. 79, p. 18.
61 *Evidence of the Engineering Employers' Federation*, para. 76, p. 9.
62 Allan Flanders, *Management and Trade Unions*, Faber, 1970, p. 58.
63 *Evidence of the Trades Union Congress*, para. 272, p. 101.
64 Minutes of Evidence, No. 30, para. 34, p. 1163.
65 *Evidence of the Confederation of British Industry*, para. 71, p. 17.
66 *Evidence of the Engineering Employers' Federation*, para. 92, p. 11.
67 *Evidence of the Confederation of British Industry*, para. 123, p. 25.
68 *Evidence of the Trades Union Congress*, para. 192, p. 75.
69 Ibid., para. 193, p. 75.
70 Minutes of Evidence, No. 30, para. 2, p. 1160.

71 Ibid., paras. 12–13, p. 1161.

72 Jeremy Bugler, 'The New Oxford Group', *New Society*, 15 February 1968.

73 The growth of workshop power was pointed out, for example, by Allan Flanders in 'Trade Unions in the Sixties', *Socialist Commentary*, August 1961, and Eric Wigham in *What's Wrong with the Unions?* Penguin, 1961.

74 'Waiting for Management', *New Society*, 20 June 1968, pp. 901–903. A more comprehensive assessment of the report is to be found in the special issue of the *British Journal of Industrial Relations*, Vol. 6, No. 3, November 1968.

75 Reforming the Voluntary System of Collective Bargaining', *The Times*, 14 June 1968.

76 The *Sunday Times*, June 1968.

77 See, for example, Eric Wigham, 'Battle of the Workers' Directors', *The Times*, 17 June 1968. Andrew Shonfield, 'Why I think we Didn't Go Far Enough', *Sunday Times*, 16 June 1968.

78 Tom Lupton, 'Can We Check the Chaos of the Outlaws and the Amateurs?' The *Sunday Times*, 16 June 1968.

79 *In Place of Strife: A Policy for Industrial Relations*, Cmnd. 3888, HMSO 1969.

80 *Report of the Royal Commission on Trade Unions and Employers' Associations: CBI/TUC Action following the Report*, 23 October 1968, Confederation of British Industry.

81 Ibid., para. 1.

82 *Report of the Royal Commission on Trade Unions and Employers' Associations: Comment by the CBI on the Report's Main Conclusions and Recommendations*, Confederation of British Industry, 7 November 1968. *Action on Donovan*, Trades Union Congress, 8 November 1968.

83 *In Place of Strife: A Policy for Industrial Relations*, Cmnd. 3888, HMSO, 1969, para. 27.

84 See the account of the intra-party fight on the Bill in Peter Jenkins, *The Battle of 10 Downing Street*, Charles Knight, 1970.

85 *Report of the Royal Commission*, para. 415, 440.

86 The *Observer*, Leader, 16 June 1968. House of Commons Debates, 17 July 1968, and Robert Carr, 'Britain's Urgent Need of a Code of Industrial Relations', *The Times*, 31 July 1968.

87 Quoted in H. A. Turner, Garfield Clack and Geoffrey Roberts, *Labour Relations in the Motor Industry*, Allen & Unwin, 1967, p. 45.

88 Ibid., p. 54.

89 *Report of the Royal Commission*, para. 415.

90 Ibid., para. 414.

91 H. A. Turner, Garfield Clack and Geoffrey Roberts, op. cit.

92 Ibid., p. 24.

93 Ibid.

94 Ibid., p. 25.

95 Ibid., p. 332.

96 Ibid., p. 54.

97 *Report of the Royal Commission*, para. 412.

98 Ibid.

99 Research Paper No. 1, *The Role of Shop Stewards in British Industrial Relations*, HMSO, 1968, p. 72.

100 Research Paper No. 10, *Shop Stewards and Workplace Relations*, HMSO, 1968.

101 Ibid., p. 56.
102 *Report of the Royal Commission*, para. 22.
103 Garfield Clack, 'How Unofficial Strikes Help Industry', *Business*, July 1965.
104 *Report of the Royal Commission*, para. 211.
105 Graham L. Reid, *An Economic Comment on the Donovan Report*, British Journal of Industrial Relations, Vol. 6, No. 3, November 1968, p. 304.
106 J. R. Crossley, *The Donovan Report: A Case Study in the Poverty of Historicism*, British Journal of Industrial Relations, Vol. 6, No. 3, November 1968, p. 298.

4 The Plowden Committee on Primary Education

MAURICE KOGAN

THE FORMAL POSITION OF THE CENTRAL ADVISORY COUNCILS FOR EDUCATION

The Secretary of State for Education and Science is required by Section 4 of the Education Act, 1944, to appoint Central Advisory Councils for Education for both England and Wales. These are meant to be continuing advisory bodies and this immediately differentiates them from the Commissions and Committees described elsewhere in this book. The Councils, in effect, replaced the Consultative Committees on Education which before the Second World War produced several famous reports – for example, the Hadow Reports on the Education of the Adolescent (1926), on Primary Education (1931 and 1933), and the Spens Report on Secondary Education (1938).[1]

The Act lays down that the CAC will 'advise the Secretary of State upon such matters connected with educational theory and practice as they think fit, and upon any questions referred to them by him' (Section 4 (1)).

So while, in law, the CACs can make their own terms of reference, or equally well have them remitted to them by the Secretary of State, in practice almost all of the famous series of CAC Reports – Early Leaving (1954), Crowther (1959), Newsom (1963), and Plowden (1967),[2] were based on terms of reference handed to the Councils by the Minister. Some of the earlier discussions and reports of the Council were based on terms of reference created by them themselves, but it was soon thought preferable by everybody concerned that the Department should take the initiative.

The same ministerial initiative is preserved by the fact that by regulations made under Section 4[3] appointments are for a period of three years and that while they are renewable – and one or two members were reappointed so as to preserve some continuity between different Councils – most members have given way to newcomers with exper-

F

tise more directly related to the new terms of reference to be followed.

The membership and the secretariat are entirely appointed by the Secretary of State. This contrasts with many bodies ostensibly appointed by him, such as the now defunct Secondary School Examinations Council and National Advisory Council for the Training and Supply of Teachers, who were formally appointed by the Secretary of State but the majority of whom were actually appointed by nomination, by the educational 'stage army' of local authority, teacher and other relevant associations. Only a few independents were appointed solely on the motion of the Minister. By contrast, the CACs, although certainly containing their share of figures well known in the education service, have been appointed from, as it were, first principles. The statutory provision is that 'Each Council shall include persons who have had experience of the statutory system of public education as well as persons who have had experience of educational institutions not forming part of that system.'*[4]

There is no easy explanation of the decision to appoint the Plowden Committee. The official announcement was made by Sir Edward Boyle in an answer to an obviously inspired Parliamentary Question from Dr Horace King on 18 June 1963. The terms of reference were 'to consider primary education in all its aspects and the transition to secondary education'. It followed a long period of discussion within the Ministry and consultation with the Treasury about its scope. The then Prime Minister, Mr Harold Macmillan, was also consulted about the chairmanship. But it resulted from no dramatic initiative from government or anyone else. The Secretary of State is bound to have Central Advisory Councils even though this fact has been ignored by successive ministers since the Plowden Committee reported and was disbanded in 1967. This being so, until Crosland decided not to re-appoint it (see page 101), officials had to find new terms of reference if only to give the Council work to do. It emerged, first of all, because something had to, but, secondly, because the CACs had studied the main components and many of the main problems of secondary and further education. Primary education was obviously overdue for study. The last official inquiry had been that of the Consultative Committee's published in 1933.

'The years following the passing of the 1944 Education Act have been a period of advance in both the resources and content of primary education. The time appears opportune for a major study of the

* The intention of this subsection is quite clear – to ensure that Councils are not packed with gifted amateurs. But whom does it exclude? Only the in-educable, it seems.

primary schools and thought about their future development.' This was how the first of the Ministry's Reports on Education (July 1963) put it. So Lady Plowden and Professor C. E. Gittins were appointed as Chairmen of the English and Welsh Councils respectively. Professor Gittins and another member of the Welsh Council (Miss Ena Grey) were members of both councils. This greatly helped the two councils to keep themselves informed of each other's thinking. The Secretary to the Welsh Council, Dr G. A. V. Morgan, HMI, attended many council and working party meetings and received all papers. He also contributed to the work of the council from the point of view of his own expertise which is in educational psychology. The Gittins Report was able to take many of the Plowden recommendations and accept or modify them. The resulting Welsh Report substantially supported the main conclusions of the Plowden Report and thus was able to concentrate on the distinctively Welsh aspects of its remit – the question of bi-lingual education, of the special problems of Welsh rural schools and so on. The two secretariats worked closely together although one was based in London and the other in Cardiff. Any student of British primary education will do well to study both reports and, indeed, students of comparative education will also find much to reward them in the comparisons between two related systems which can be drawn from the two reports.*

THE DEVELOPING ROLE OF THE CENTRAL ADVISORY COUNCILS

That the Plowden Committee was appointed as part of a regular and ongoing official process rather than as the result of strong public or professional pressure is neither surprising nor reprehensible. The CACs were evidently devised to provide a continuing, ruminative and contemplative service to the Department of Education and Science and to the education service and no dramatic results have ever been expected from the Reports. None has been given terms of reference resulting from sharp political or public pressure. Within the education service, they may be contrasted with the Robbins Committee, a Committee set up by the Prime Minister – and appointed in response to sophisticated public demand for an enquiry into the future of higher education. Robbins produced recommendations that changed – within a decade – the whole landscape of higher education. The appointment of the Robbins' Committee by Macmillan evidently resulted from a govern-

---

* The Gittins Report is contained in a single volume of 646 pages. It was also translated into Welsh by four professors of Welsh.

The two councils were given identical terms of reference but this essay will concern itself only with the English Council – the Plowden Committee.

ment intention to permit, if not indeed to encourage, radical rethinking about the size, functions and organisation of such sacred institutions as universities.

The CACs have never had that type of role. Nor have they had the almost quasi-judicial type of role of, say, the Wolfenden Committee on Homosexual Offences and Prostitution, or the Fulton Committee on the Civil Service (if we dare mention both in the same sentence). One of these tested the equity and usefulness of a piece of social control while the other held up for review a part of the system of public administration. Both of these were under quite specific political and other challenges at the time that the committees were established.

The CACs have had instead the function of summing up practices in education and the present state of progress as seen at the time that the Reports were written, for the government, for educational practitioners, for the education service, and for the community in general, and of identifying problems and needs. The Reports have thus had a mixture of objectives and of outcomes that account for what some would regard as the inordinate length of some of the Reports. The Councils could hardly meet the demands made on them in less space.

An examination of the four Reports that preceded Plowden will show how these quite mixed purposes were met. The Reports have, first, an evangelical role: they provide teachers and teacher trainers with examples of the best practices in the area of education being studied. Look, for example, at the roseate picture of the English sixth form in Crowther,[5] or of practical work in secondary modern schools in Newsom[6] or of the freedom and flexibility of 'open schooling' in primary schools in Plowden[7]. The Reports all contain exhortatory writing which has relied on the best to be found in the schools by Her Majesty's Inspectors of Schools and others who have advised the Councils. There is, it is not unfair to say, a decided tendency not to describe *the worst* that can be found. These are not reports that attack abuse. They encourage the best by describing it.

Secondly, the Reports have all mounted arguments for changes in policy which were already being mooted within the education and wider social service world. 'Early Leaving'[8] made a judicious review of how and why some of our best talent seeps away because too many people leave school at fifteen years, and made specific recommendations. The Report recommended that there should be an end to the practice of requiring grammar school pupils' parents to sign agreements that they would not leave school before the age of sixteen and instead to do something about giving them adequate allowances which would make it easier for poorer parents to keep their children at school. The Crowther Report, among many important recommendations, provided powerful arguments for raising the age of compulsory schooling to sixteen – all the more powerful because the Report rehearsed the arguments for and against and also brought in the full weight of educational economics.[9]

The Plowden Report contained 197 recommendations. They included the provision of universal nursery education, the changing of the compulsory ages of entry to full-time education and of transfer to junior (or middle) and secondary education, the creation of educational priority areas and many other important recommendations. Many of these recommendations were already being evolved within the education service. But the Plowden Report picked them up, studied them, added the weight of evidence from the education service and from research, and codified them into a plan for a better, if not a revolutionised, primary education service. Some proposals were new. Others had been the stock in trade of education conferences for twenty years.

Finally, these reports between them came at precisely the right time to legitimise new thinking about the relation between education and society and, particularly, to reinforce current changes in official thinking about selectivity in all stages of education. The Reports of the Consultative Committees and of such other Committees as the Secondary School Examinations Council which produced the Norwood Report (1943) had performed much the same function before the war. These Reports advanced the case for systems by which pupils were selected according to ability and also were concerned with the techniques of selecting them. The authors of the Report were implicitly concerned with ensuring that the able poor got a fair chance in life. By the mid-1950s educational sociologists had renounced what Anthony Crosland[10] called the 'weak concept of equality'. In talking about the CACs later (1971), Crosland agreed that: 'The CAC did document the good and the bad of the system and, in particular, legitimised the radical sociology of the fifties and sixties. Better than any other group of documents.'[11] This role perhaps emerges as one of the most important. The Department of Education and Science or the Ministry of Education was, in the late 1940s, and throughout the fifties and much of the sixties, one of the few government departments that put resources into development work.* Its Architects and Building Branch and Teacher Supply Branch became fine examples of how a government department could put resources and effort into advancing its own knowledge and the knowledge of its service, and of how to improve the system that it administered. But government departments find it as difficult as any other organisations to take account of all of the movements with which they have to interact, particularly when some of the external forces are necessarily in conflict with the policies being enunciated by govern-

* The Defence and Supply Departments have always done this, of course.

ment at the time. Thus in the 1950s and 1960s several educational and social developments were at work and the department was slow to catch up with some of them. Some, indeed, were already part of the progressive policies enunciated by the Ministry and by Her Majesty's Inspectors of Schools. For example, the child-centred educational theories which were so eloquently stated in the Hadow reports in the 1930s were carried forward by the work of HM Inspectors in the schools, and in-service courses, and so on. They were worked out in more detail, with more evidence from the field, and over broader fronts in the Newsom, Crowther and Plowden Reports. A second theme was never fully taken up by the official committees largely because it was, and still is, a fighting point between the main political parties – the substitution of comprehensive education for selective systems of education. The third theme was that of education as a 'distributor of life chances'[12] – the assumption being that education had a distributive function and that one of its roles was to redress social equality. This argument was carried out throughout the 1950s and 1960s in surprisingly muted tones, almost as a technical argument between the educational psychologists who in the 1920s and 1930s had done so much to substantiate the weak concept of equality – that all children should have a chance to be educated to the level of their discoverable ability – and the sociologists and psychologists who in the 1950s were showing that educational testing was inaccurate, that selective systems placed a premium on a child's social background, and that the waste of ability was enormous.

Such doctrines as these, of radical educational sociology, were not only written into the CAC Reports but were legitimised by them. And successive CACs enabled some of the important original work on these problems to be undertaken by such as Gilbert Peaker (an HMI) who provided most of the data for CACs on early leaving, on reading ability and on the ways in which social factors affected secondary modern school pupils' performance. This work was directly commissioned and encouraged by the CACs. It is doubtful whether the Ministry of Education, left to itself, would have undertaken it.

Indeed, the Councils not only brought in, or legitimised, thinking otherwise unlikely to arise from ordinary process of government – they were in a better position than the Ministry to absorb and make sense of the work of academics of the generations at work while they made their studies. They also reflected well, and to some extent anticipated, ideological conflicts and consensuses. Plowden was the first report to state the principle that public authorities should exercise 'positive discrimination'[13] in favour of the under-priviledged. This conclusion was reached at precisely the point in time when the controversy about universality and selectivity was being mounted by Richard Titmuss[14] and others. It was, curiously enough, a doctrine that could appeal to both the universalists and the selectivists on the council.

A careful reader of the CAC reports would thus find them important source materials for the political and ideological history of the periods in which they were written. In the main they were slightly in advance of official opinion; the tug boats of gradualist radicalism.

THE PRESSURES FOR AND AGAINST PLOWDEN

It will be seen, then, that the Plowden Committee was not established to evaluate a contentious issue, or to make specific recommendations on the reform of a system felt generally to need reform, but evolved from a statutory provision made with a quite general intention to ensure that ministers were informed of how the best opinion viewed the education service and its problems over time.

No parliamentary questions had been asked seeking an enquiry into primary education for at least some years before the Committee was appointed, although questions had been asked concerning some of the main issues which the Committee discussed – such as the lifting of restrictions on nursery education.

If there was no pressure for its establishment, there was a spontaneous, and as far as one can judge, genuine welcome for its establishment. A few newspapers niggled.

The *Daily Express* (19 June 1963) wrote that 'Too often educational ideas are accepted because their supporters are vocal and influential. Now these theories are to be put to the test. Be stern, Sir Edward! And judge purely by the results.' *The Guardian* pointed out that Boyle's announcement had been overshadowed by the Profumo affair but thought the appointment of the Committee a move of major importance. *The Times* sat on both sides of the fence in warning against a report that would not be too expository for teachers as had been the Crowther Report, but which would trim unattainable ideas. 'We need a firm appraisal of priorities.' In spite of these warnings, however, it thought the Report would be the primary schools' Robbins Report. The *Times Educational Supplement* (16 August) objected to the omission of members from the Incorporated Association of Preparatory Schools and secondary modern schools, a point that coincidentally had been urged repeatedly by the Deputy Chairman to the Council, John Newsom, to all who would listen to him.

There were some criticisms about the establishment of the Plowden Committee but they were few, idiosyncratic, and were really requests for more rather than for less. One critic, the militant National

Association of School Masters, wanted a Royal Commission rather than a mere Central Advisory Council inquiry into primary education.[15] The same body objected to a study of the education service through piece-meal inquiries into different areas.

The general enthusiasm matched well the perking up of interest in primary education in the earlier 1960s. One contribution was personal and political – Edward Boyle who established the Committee had, particularly during his period as Parliamentary Secretary, brought his own charismatic force and interest in educational issues as such, which distinguished him from other ministers, to bear on the problems and achievements of primary education. He was unashamedly interested in promoting curriculum development, in such issues as the retention or rejection of streaming in primary schools[16] as was shown in one or two of his parliamentary speeches and in many of his speeches around the country as a junior minister. In the early 1960s, too, the Nuffield Foundation made the first of the philanthropoid moves in this country towards creating development projects in primary education – in science, mathematics, and foreign language teaching. The short-lived Curriculum Study Group in the Ministry of Education* listed such areas as primary school science, mathematics, and modern language teaching in the first list of problems it intended to study. Educational psychology and sociology happened, at that time, to be paying particular interest to primary education – the work of J. W. B. Douglas[17] and of Basil Bernstein[18] was catching up on the studies made by Halsey and Floud[19] and others in secondary education.

The Committee was welcomed but was, in fact, taken more seriously by the educationists and by the public generally than by the Department which appointed and serviced it. Eight years later Anthony Crosland, the minister who received the report in 1967, stated that 'the Department didn't much like the CAC'.[20] Crosland's reception of it, in his Preface† to the Report and in his reply to a debate in Parliament on it, was somewhat tepid.[21] And members of the Council felt, although they were too polite to say so while the Council was sitting, that during its existence the Department did not give it the moral support or follow

* Established a year before the Plowden Committee was appointed by David Eccles with the job of 'foreseeing changes before they happened'. It was killed by the suspicions of the teachers' associations but was intended to be a resource to the CAC.

† The Council were thanked for their 'thoroughness'. 'The many recommendations in the Report, some of far-reaching significance, will be studied with the greatest care by the Government and the work done by the Council, with so much diligence and public spirit, will enable decisions to be reached on a more informed basis by those who are charged with securing the best development of English education within the resources available.'

it with the interest they felt it deserved, although they would be the first to say that the DES supplied all the data they asked for without stint.

The reasons for this reluctant acceptance by the Department are complex and cannot be tactfully stated, let alone properly documented. One of them might have been a persistent reluctance by government and the DES to take seriously its own role as promoter of educational policy. For a long while after the 1944 Act, the Department considered itself not as an educational planning department, or as leaders on policy, but primarily as a mediator between the 'real' agents of educational government – the local education authorities, the teachers and the denomination and the government-wide network of control and economic policy lead by the Treasury.[22] Some of the changes in that attitude have already been mentioned. When Boyle ceased to be Minister in October, 1964, and while his successors, and particularly Crosland, in no sense renounced the leadership role – indeed, under Crosland it reached a new and different dimension – the Department's interest in curriculum and education as such receded and there was a perceptible decline in the developmental approach to them – partly it is true because of the establishment of the Schools' Council in 1964. This may have been because of the appointment from other departments of the two most senior officials – the Permanent and Deputy Secretary – responsible for schools' policy.

And other and more complex forces were at work. The Department had its own policy priorities and did not particularly welcome powerful and thrusting encouragement from one of its own advisory councils. Thus, the Department had already decided to loosen the legal restrictions on the creation of middle schools,* and, with it, the passing of the 1964 Education Act. Yet this proposal was central to the Council's studies. Equally, Anthony Crosland's Circular 10/65 which 'requested' local authorities to submit plans for comprehensive education again vitally affected the Plowden Committee's thinking about the age of transition from primary to secondary education – an explicit part of their terms of reference. The Committee later devoted a long, complex and sophisticated chapter to the different alternatives (Chapter 10). An active Minister like Crosland could well find an active Council under a vigorous Chairman such as Lady Plowden, something of a nuisance. In 1971, while conceding the value of the reports, Crosland said, '. . . but there's a danger of too many and too lengthy reports. And they

* The 1964 Education Act enabled schools to be established which cut across the legal definements that there should be separate schools for primary education (from three to eleven or twelve years), and for secondary education (from eleven or twelve to eighteen years).

can slow up action, as Plowden would have done on comprehensive reorganisation if I hadn't been firm. . . .'[23] In fact, Lady Plowden would almost certainly have made sure that the Council's thinking did not slow up action. But Crosland was not to know this.

Leaving aside the tensions caused by the relationship between this particular Council and the Department which, at that time, had immediate preoccupations placed on it by an active minister, there are structural issues – concerning the way in which a Department formulates its policies – which vitally affected the role of the Plowden Committee. This point will be discussed later.

METHODS OF WORK

The Committee's methods of work were largely affected by its membership. It was appointed with twenty-three members but, at its own request, further members were appointed to bring in expertise from the secondary modern school and the private primary school areas. The membership was unusual inasmuch as it contained, not only a lay Chairman, and a Deputy Chairman (Sir John Newsom) who was formerly a chief education officer, an educational publisher and Chairman of the previous CAC, but a wider range of interests than previous Committees. There were four practising primary head and assistant head teachers and two heads of secondary schools'* There were two chief inspectors. There was a local authority educational psychologist. There were two former Chairmen of education committees. The big change was in the introduction of a group of academics. These included A. J. Ayer, the Wykeham Professor of Logic at Oxford, David Donnison, Professor of Social Administration at the LSE, and the sociologist, Michael Young, J. M. Tanner, Reader (later Professor) in Child Growth and Development at London University, and Ian Byatt, an economist from the London School of Economics. There was also a leading Principal from the teacher education world – Molly Brearley. Two other interesting additions were the Editor of *New Society*, Timothy Raison, and two representatives of parents – one from the Confederation for the Advancement of State Education.

In appointing this 'non-educational' group; both Edward Boyle and those who advised him were obviously concerned that the Report should not only contain the best opinions of the education service but also show how the primary schools might be viewed from the point of view of the social and biological sciences more generally, as well as from the somewhat more objective point of view that might be expected from

* One of them, Eric Hawkins, is now a professor of modern language teaching.

a leading exponent of logical positivism,* or the progressive conservatism of Tim Raison.

The Council was served by a full-time team consisting of a Secretary and an Assistant Secretary who were a Principal and Higher Executive Officer from the DES, an HMI as main educational adviser, an ILEA School Inspector and, for a shorter time, another HMI. There were two principal DES assessors – the Under Secretary in charge of Schools' Branch and the Chief Inspector for Primary Education – and a larger number of specialists from different parts of the Department – a medical officer, a statistician, many HMIs, architects and administrators from different branches were available to produce information and views on any point asked for. This large group advised the Council directly or through its working parties.

By any standards the Council was too large. This was because of its multiplicity of objectives – to ensure that educational opinion was fully represented and yet subject to effective criticism or support from non-educationists. There were also problems in organising its work, in getting all members to participate fully. There was too much of a burden on the secretariat, and also general discomfort, particularly since the DES Headquarters in Curzon Street House has only two rooms which are capable of housing a council of twenty-five and its advisers. And, during much of the Council's period of life, at least one of those rooms reverberated to the sound of workmen demolishing the façade put up to protect Field Marshal Montgomery who used the building as part of his headquarters during the war.

In practice, the Council remitted much of its detailed work to working parties and study groups. There were separate study groups for visits to different parts of the country and to other countries. The working parties studied such detailed aspects of the terms of reference as the growth and development of children, the social factors affecting primary education, the overall organisation of primary education and the transition to secondary education, the curriculum and internal organisation of primary schools, the training of primary school teachers, the economics, finance and research programmes of primary education. Other smaller teams looked at problems of school building and design and the special problems of handicapped children. Each of these working parties met a large number of times and received and generated a large number of papers. They produced reports to the Council which became incorporated in the main Report.

The Council visited twenty-three English local authorities, 289

* Sir Alfred Ayer will be the first to agree, however, that his professional pursuit of philosophy did not inhibit him from having strong opinions about many of the issues, educational and otherwise, discussed by the Committee.

schools,* universities and colleges, and also paid short visits to Russia, Poland, Denmark, Sweden, France and the U.S.A. It had a total of some 116 days of meetings and visits but even this figure is no true account of the committed time because travel to and from a half-day meeting, and preparation for a meeting, also added to the burden of members. One member has written that his duties kept him out of school two days a week in term-time.[24] Some 465 papers were written and the list of evidence, solicited or otherwise, which was received, fills seventeen pages. No member was paid for this work and travel and subsistence allowances were at the usual thin government service level.†

Throughout this period enthusiasm was sustained and the Council's meetings were extremely well attended. A strong camaraderie developed among members and with the secretariat, and much of this must be attributed to the Chairman's driving and positive interest which held the Council together. Yet as one looks at those criticisms of the Council's work (see, for example, R. S. Peters, 1969),[25] some of which accurately discern the Committee's unawareness of some aspects of the theories they discussed, one has to ask whether so large a burden should have been placed on so heterogeneous and large a body. Throughout, the full-time officials were seriously overworked and many of the issues unresolved by the Report could have been better tackled were there more leisure with which to study them and less pressure generated by the need to service so large and varied a Council.

For the most part, the Council's working methods were those traditional to government commissions although there were a few significant differences from previous CACs. The secretariat prepared the main papers in which data were put together, conclusions suggested and new lines of exploration proposed. The Council or its working parties considered the papers and authorised draft reports to the Council and draft chapters of the whole Report. Almost all of the first drafts of chapters were written by one or other members of the secretariat (with one or two notable exceptions where the content was of a highly technical and scientific nature): these were written by a member of the Council. Some chapters were barely changed while others were substantially written and rewritten by members of the Council and, perhaps, by the secretariat again. The Chairman throughout the life of the Council made the main decisions on the shape of the Report and on its style of writing although she did not herself draft chapters. On such strategic issues as the age at which children should enter and leave the different stages of primary education, the Chairman herself put

* Including a few in Scotland.
† They travelled first-class but taxis were not generally permitted. A 24-hour absence entitled them to £3·15 subsistence allowance. (September 1965 figures).

together the arguments, including some extremely detailed technical arguments, and DES officials and HMIs contributed to several decisions, while preserving their correct distance from the Council. At no time was pressure put on the CAC who were, in any case, anxious to produce a 'useful' report that the DES could hope to implement.

The making of the Report differed from previous CAC reports in several respects. First, the DES sought and received agreement from the Government for a large research programme which powerfully affected some at least of the Committee's conclusions. Researches were undertaken by members of the secretariat, HMIs, the Government Social Survey division of the COI working closely with two HMIs, Miss Stella Duncan and Gilbert Peaker, by Professor Stephen Wiseman (Univeristy of Manchester), the NFER, Dr G. Baron and Mr D. Howell of the London University Institute of Education Unit on School Management and Government of Education, Mr Bleddyn Davies, the Research Division of the Ministry of Housing and Local Government, the National Child Development Study, and three researchers from different universities, Mr (now Professor) A. T. Collis, Mrs Julia Parker and Mr D. Miller on the social services affecting primary school children.*

In order to get this research programme off the ground and back again to the Council in time for decisions on the main recommendations, the secretariat had to work fast. They were appointed a few months before the Chairman or the Council and by the time the Council met in the autumn of 1963, proposals for at least one of the most important pieces of research – the 1964 National Survey of School, Parental Attitudes, and Circumstances Related to School and Pupil Characteristics – had been prepared so that the Council, and particularly its expert working party under David Donnison, could rapidly decide whether to ask the Social Survey, HMIs, and others to make the necessary starts. Almost all of the research findings were received in time for the main drafting of the report which began in the early months of 1966. Much of the initial design was undertaken by the remarkably able HMI who worked full-time with the Committee – Stella Duncan.

The use made of research by the Council was not always what would be acceptable to some researchers but it seems perfectly legitimate to this author. All research findings were written up fully in Vol. 2 and referred to appropriately in Vol. 1. But the Council did not scruple to follow the judgement of its own members, and of the weight of non-research evidence from its witnesses, rather than follow the results of such research findings as that which 'showed' that, for example, schools with large classes produce 'better' school performance than those with

* These researches are reported in Vol. 2 of the Report.

smaller classes or that 'formal' education produces 'better' results than informal education.[26] (There are good reasons why these research results are valid but not decisive to the issues being argued.) In such cases the Council accepted the onus of arguing with the research evidence when it could not accept it.* In other parts of the Council's Report the research reinforced judgements of impression. For example, the place of parental attitudes in children's performances was clearly brought out by the regression and other analyses of the National Survey Data recorded in Appendices 3 and 4. This research was early seen by the secretariat as a key area which needed further study on the basis of the somewhat intuitive findings of earlier researches such as those of Elizabeth Fraser,[27] and Floud, Halsey and Martin.[28]

This last example also demonstrates how research led to the important recommendations in Chapter 4 of the Report about the relationships between school and home and the way in which schools ought to build up a policy for parental participation.† These recommendations have had some effect (although not as much as might be desired) but they were among the earlier statements about the influence of client participation in social service institutions – an issue likely to be explosive and already beginning to tick in the early 1970s. Other research – on the way in which the primary schools relate to social services – led to the recommendations in Chapter 7 that later fed into the Seebohm Report which was being written at that time. Indeed, the careful reader will find in paragraphs 240 and 248 of Plowden the concept of the Area Team which has been a fundamental concept of both the Seebohm Report[29] and the 1970 Act[30] which followed it.

Other researches were also important. Chapters 4 to 7 of the Report about the social factors affecting primary education, the creation of the policy of positive discrimination through the creation of educational priority areas, were able to rest not only on the Council's research but also on the substantial findings of educational sociologists of the previous decade. The Council was able to get pre-publication copies of such works as J. W. B. Douglas's *Home and School*[31], upon which it relied extensively. At the same time, the environmentalist findings of sociologists could be balanced against the somewhat more biologically determined views of the child development experts. Chapter 2 of the Plowden Report is a skilful mid-way statement between the two.

* 'Although positive evidence from research in favour of small classes is lacking, this does not outweigh professional advice, public opinion and the example of other countries.' (para. 86)

† This research, so important to the Committee's proposals, has been held up to learned scrutiny. Jean Floud in *The Teacher*, 10 Feb 1967, found the design, and hence the conclusions, limited.

So research findings had an important part to play in the writing of the Report. Where the Report did not depend well on research, it identified gaps in knowledge.[32] But there were, too, large areas of its remit that were not well researched, so that discussion of some of the more controversial issues was a bit blurred. Thus, the predominantly child-centred and Froebelian flavour of the Report, derived from thirty or so years of experience of the primary schools, was powerfully presented to the Committee through a large amount of evidence, much of it impressionistic, and gained from visits to schools as well as from the written statements from HMIs and other witnesses. This type of thinking could not easily be reconciled with some of the early findings of, say, Basil Bernstein[33] some of whose data appeared in the Council's offices on the day that the final text was being cleared with the printers. Bernstein emphasised the importance of verbal codes developed in the home. If one were to take his findings to their logical conclusion, as some of the American attempts to reverse deprivation by operant conditioning have done, children would be exposed to programmes of verbal and other reinforcement which would be in conflict with 'learning through discovery' under the informal guidance of teachers. Plowden was anxious that there should be maximum freedom for both teacher and pupil, this being a key feature of British primary education, and that educational procedures should only be structured so as to ensure that a rich environment was created in which children could find their own way. Such issues as this begin with discussions of a technical nature but can powerfully affect policy as any comparison of the role structure of a British with, say, French or Swedish primary school will show. The Committee did not, and could not, take all of these issues on board. Time, its own composition, and the state of research in these areas, were all against it.

There has been sophisticated criticism of the use made of research by the Plowden Committee.[34] But the critics would agree that the Council at least made a conscientious effort to commission what research could be performed in time and to use the findings as well as they could be used.

The second novel feature of the committee's work has already been referred to. The mix of its membership undoubtedly affected the breadth of its studies. While somewhat over half of the Report is concerned with 'education' proper, large sections of the Report are concerned with the developmental and social aspects. Other chapters on the government of primary education, its status, on school building, and so on, demonstrate the range that was attempted.

A further new characteristic of the Council and of its Report can be found in Chapter 31. Here the Council attempted to show the financial and legal consequences of their findings, to put cost figures on them, and to express priorities. There is even a time table for implementation. They also attempted to discuss more generally the cost and benefits of primary education. This proved to be an extraordinary intractable subject and the attempt demonstrates, perhaps, the hypnotic effect that economics was then beginning to exercise over educational thinking.

These differences in style and content of report-making and writing have not been widely followed. The Fulton Committee, for example, did not cost its recommendations. And other social service departments still appoint large committees whose members are mainly drawn from the area of activity being examined. Indeed, in appointing the James Committee on teacher education the DES seem to have learnt the need for full-time work, but have gone almost wholly over to a membership of those directly or indirectly concerned with teacher education. They also assumed that further research was not needed. One of the lessons of the Plowden Report, and of the mixture of membership that Boyle brought into it, was that there are advantages in not having Committees of cavalry officers assessing the advantages of the tank.

Before discussing the effects of the Report, it will be convenient to summarise its main recommendations. One group of recommendations confirm the role of parents in the school by proposing that schools create programmes for contact with children's homes. Parents and other adults were to be invited to participate in school activities, and the concept of 'community schools' was commended.

It confirmed the development of a national policy of 'positive discrimination' whereby schools in neighbourhoods where children were most severely handicapped by home conditions should be declared educational priority areas. Special resources of staff, buildings and money were to be made available to them.

There were recommendations about the way in which schools should relate to health and social services through a grouping of existing organisations that would include social workers 'largely responsible for school social work' (Vol. I, para. 255 (ii)). This was an important precursor of the Seebohm recommendations for area teams but emphasised the need for specialist work on educational problems.

Several recommendations concerned the organisation of primary education. There should be a large expansion of nursery education which was to be paid for by a relaxation of the law concerning the age at which children must attend school full-time. Children should begin school gradually and only become full-timers when they were ready, as individuals, to cope with a whole day of schooling. The schools should offer a three-year course in the first school and a four-year course in the middle school. But generally there should be flexibility for individuals in their entry to school and transfer between the different stages of education.

The Report commended the use of selection procedures other than 'externally imposed intelligence and attainment tests' in those areas where authorities continued to insist on selection procedures (para. 415).

The Report concerned itself with the optimum size of primary schools (a first school to be of 240 children and a middle school to be of 300 to 450 children). Special arrangements might apply to rural areas (para. 467).

The Report contained several chapters on curriculum and internal organisation of schools. The Committee wanted recurring national surveys of attainment similar to those undertaken on reading by the Department of Education. There were strong divisions within the Committee on religious education but no attempt, by the majority, to seek a repeal of the law requiring children to attend religious education and acts of worship.

It was recommended that the infliction of physical pain as a method of punishment in primary schools should be forbidden and that independent schools which continued to inflict physical pain as a recognised method of punishment should not be registered.

Schools should be organised flexibly so as to provide a combination of individual groups and classwork and the trend towards individual learning should be encouraged. Flexibility in the length of the school day and the spacing of the school year should also be encouraged. The Report discouraged 'streaming' (division into groups according to the ability of children) in the infants school and hoped it would continue to spread into the junior school. There were careful recommendations about the staffing of schools. Apart from a need for more generous staffing the Committee was concerned with the development of better conditions for part-time service, for help to teachers through assistants, secretaries and for trained teachers' aids. It was suggested that there need be a general review of advisory services (a need which becomes more obvious as time goes on). And the Committee recommended that there should be a full inquiry into the system of training teachers. This recommendation has been followed up by the appointment of a full-time committee, the James Committee, which is looking into the structure of the training system.

There were detailed recommendations about the training of nursery assistants and teachers' aids who would make it possible for there to be a major expansion in nursery education and a reduction in the workload of individual teachers.

G

The Committee asked for the application of more stringent criteria for the registration of independent schools.

There were recommendations about the improvement of primary school buildings – not all of which suggested the use of extra money. One of the recommendations read: 'The Department should undertake a careful study of present requirements for nursery education which may well be lavish in some respects.'(para. 113 (v)).

There was an important chapter on the status and government of primary education. The Committee stated that primary school teachers should be represented on local education committees and sub-committees. There was concern that the present somewhat muddled status and functions of school managers should be clarified. It was recommended that there should be representatives on the managing body of parents of children attending the school. (This recommendation has since been followed by the Inner London Education Authority.)

The last of the recommendations read 'All unecessary and unjustified differences of treatment between primary and secondary education should be eliminated' (para. 1150 (xxi)).

There was, in fact, hardly a concern of the primary schools that was omitted. The Report contains chapters on the education of handicapped children and of gifted children. The heart of the Report is concerned with the educational content of the curriculum for normal children but this is paralleled by the major recommendations for the special arrangements to be made for deprived children. Much of the Report is concerned not simply with the merits of the proposals made but with their feasibility and their costs. While many of the recommendations were directed towards the Department, many more were directed towards the teaching profession, parents, and the community at large in the hope that attitudes as well as policies would change.

EFFECTS OF THE REPORT

The Report was received on the day of publication and immediately afterwards with acclamation by the main associations and the press, although there were inevitably some reservations. *The School Government Chronicle*[35] complained of its length and of its price. It was also fearful of the cost of implementing the main recommendations. The *Daily Telegraph* wrote that 'the report displays some of the worst features of official expert enquiries into aspects of social policy. Far from applying the tests of objective science to the conclusions of current prejudice, it merely reproduces the prejudice.' It described the policy of positive discrimination as 'merely another expression of contemporary egalitarian dogma, the view that at every point the interests of those who have shown themselves capable of benefiting from education should be subordinated to those who show no wish to receive it'. The *Financial Times* described the proposals as 'sensible and necessary, if somewhat expensive'. 'New School Charter', 'Childrens' Charter', 'The Classroom Revolution' were headlines in the popular press. *The Times* and The *Guardian* were gingerly approving. Edward Boyle was reported as saying that the Report was all he had hoped for.

Forty thousand copies of Volume I were sold in one month and a total of 146,000 copies had been sold (excluding those issued for official purposes) by the end of October 1971. More surprisingly, nearly 22,000 copies of Volume 2 – a hefty volume of research findings – have been sold.

The results have been of several kinds. The deepest disappointment has been the government's failure to undertake any *systematic* follow up of its own Council's findings. Crosland[36] states that 'We set up a special working group inside the department to go through all the recommendations in minute detail, but their work wasn't finished by the time I left. As you know, I made a rather anodyne speech in the House of Commons welcoming the Report when it came out, and later a speech to the NUT . . . accepting certain parts of the Report on the management of schools and things like that. I had a lot of work going on inside the Department and it was one of the things which I was coming back to in the autumn of 1966. . . .'

In fact, Crosland accepted the general conclusions on the establishment of educational priority areas while almost wholly ignoring the criteria and mechanisms proposed by the Council. And while he might have been a bit short of time in which to follow up the Report, he was not all that short. The draft Report had been seen by officials as it was written and a virtually final copy was in their hands in the summer of 1967. It was physically handed to Crosland, in return for a glass of sherry, by Lady Plowden at the end of October 1967 – some ten months before he left the DES. With much the same processes, it had proved possible to accept the recommendations of the Robbins Report on the day of publication. Crosland's successor, Edward Short, had nearly three years of office in which to pursue the recommendations further. The official reception of the 197 recommendations is all the more baffling because of the Council's conscientious attempt to make their recommendations uncostly. Thus it proposed not additional resources for educational priority areas or for an expansion of nursery education, but a diversion of resources from what they felt to be the educationally unsound provision for full-time education for all children from the age of five onwards. The policies for parent participation, for improving social service collaboration, for continuous surveys into reading and other forms of ability, for reform of school management, for lengthening the first school period, would have required considerable expenditure of forethought and energy by the Department but hardly more resources. Such key recommendations as an improvement in in-service training for teachers would have cost money but would have been extremely cheap in comparison with other government-sponsored proposals, of far less importance to the build-up of a public service.

So as an immediate planning and social engineering exercise, Plowden scored no great success. Its success lies in other and less easy to define fields. First, it undoubtedly reinforced and strengthened the liberating effects of progressive education in a large number of schools – this being the evidence of HMIs who have assessed the results of the Report over time. It has succeeded in its evangelical purpose.

The second and wholly unexpected result has been its impact abroad, and particularly in the U.S.A. On the basis of Plowden, a large number of American visitors have sought to describe, explain, and emulate the 'British infants school' or the 'British open school'. One superb commentary written by Joseph Featherstone in the *New Republic*, 1968,[37] sold 100,000 off-prints. Some States have officially adopted the British primary school in the terms described in the Plowden Report and there has been a sudden rush of writing on the subject. The results of such adoptions are probably best not contemplated since the model is so inarticulately stated in Plowden and elsewhere that the American systems' installers might have difficulty in deciding what they are emulating.[38] Historians of cultural transfer will find something here to follow up.

Finally, there has been a quiet 'ripple' effect – not only have schools followed the examples given but surely many more teachers, parents and students have become aware of the existence of a remarkable phenomenon in the British social services as well as of what are now the commonplaces of educational sociology and developmental theory.

PLOWDEN AND THE MACHINERY OF GOVERNMENT

In retrospect there are several lessons to be learned from the Plowden example. First, the CAC mechanism – of long-term assessment of parts of the educational service – is only likely to be directly useful to government (leaving aside its usefulness in the ways indicated above) if there is a prior decision by government that the service ought to be assessed and the results of the assessment taken seriously. Ministers in a hurry can advance on the most superficial or ignore the most careful findings of any inquiry. This being so, it seems likely that if it is to be resurrected the CAC ought to be tied up much more closely with the DES planning mechanisms.[39] Here the model is the Swedish Commission which consider problems put to it, in policy terms, by government and produces 'answers' which can be taken seriously.

Secondly, if this formula is followed, something will have to be done about membership. The uneasy compromise between expert membership and representatives of the various interests has to be broken down perhaps by allowing expert Commissions to get on with the work which is then submitted by government to review by the professional bodies, or by some other device. Twenty-five people and a small secretariat cannot cope with the multiplicity of objectives and pressures put on such a body as Plowden. Thirdly, however, any such device requires the DES to be clearer about its objectives in the areas where study is needed. Its policy and activity review mechanisms should make this possible. Finally, the dependence of the secretariat upon the DES needs to be considered. If CACs are overtly part of government machinery, the secretariat can be dependent on the DES and the Civil Service for their careers. If, however, the secretariat is to take on a role of genuine independence, the duality created by loyalty to a CAC, which might be in conflict with the Department where promotion lies, ought to be avoided. This is not to say that the DES has been at all beastly to the administrators who served the CACs. On the contrary, two former secretaries to the CAC are now Deputy Secretaries in the DES. But it is a rough period of one's career to live through.

The CACs are now, illegally, in abeyance. Crosland never intended to reappoint them and Edward Short and Margaret Thatcher have not done so. Crosland said in 1971[40]: 'The Reports grew longer and longer, and more and more monumental and took up more and more of the time of already hard-worked officials. . . . I haven't taken a final decision but I think I would have reappointed it once more for a fairly quick inquiry into teacher training, and then sought a change of law enabling it to be disbanded as a permanent body. . . . We've got to the point now where the general theme of educational and social background . . . has been taken in and it doesn't need more inquiries to drive it home. We've got a large body now of active educationists who can carry this discussion on themselves. The point of having outside committees should now be to inquire into more precise and specific issues.' Edward Boyle,[41] speaking at the time, took a different view: 'I was personally sorry when it ceased to exist and nothing put in its place. The discipline of an *ad hoc* body sitting for some time is considerable. . . . It isn't only the report. If you read the evidence given to Robbins . . . they are fascinating reading. Much of Plowden's is of the same order. The research on what makes a good school – parental attitudes and the other variables – and the whole of the second volume is important stuff.'

Crosland's view was contrary to conventional wisdom and, as with everything from that source, it is worth considering carefully. To criticise it first: how would educational sociology have found its way into official acceptance if CACs had not applied it in four successive Reports? The Councils, including Plowden, turned the radical sociology of nearly ten years into conventional wisdom. Might not this be true of other facts and views of the education service? For example, might we not expect the recently created but terribly messy higher education system to produce problems and issues in the next decade that should be reviewed by those outside the government that itself creates the system? Would we be safe in assuming that the DES, left to itself, would undertake such reviews? It did *not* do so with most of the issues tackled by the CACs. Crosland's scepticism about the methodology is well founded. There is, however, a danger in assuming that because the CAC formula was not particularly successful, one need not search vigorously for alternative formulas. No one is doing that now.

From this essay it will be plain that the origins or impressions on the Plowden Committee are not easily described by any political or scientific model. There was little pressure for its appointment, a lot of spontaneous enthusiasm for its findings – the subject is important to every citizen with young children – but no coherent pattern of action on or reaction to its conclusions. It most usefully throws up questions of how government departments, inevitably headed by Ministers of short political life span, can review fundamental policies in the light of developments of general, professional, and social scientific and other technological opinion and knowledge. The attitude of the Government on this issue has been cyclical. First, it kept clear of the external intelligentsia in formulating policy and preferred well-established members of the educational professions to gently assess themselves. Then, with Robbins and Plowden it went strongly the other way. Now it is seeking to strengthen its intelligence services through internal planning arrangements largely undertaken without external help. There needs to be some balance between these three different methods.

NOTES

1 Report of the Consultative Committee on the Education of the Adolescent, 1926.
  Report of the Consultative Committee on the Primary School, 1931.
  Report of the Consultative Committee on Infant and Nursery Schools, 1933.
  Report on Secondary Education, 1938.

2 Reports of the Central Advisory Council for Education (England), HMSO. 'Early Leaving', 1954.
'15 to 18', 1959, (Crowther), 2 Vols.
'Half Our Future', 1963, (Newsom).
'Children and Their Primary Schools', 1967, (Plowden,) 2 vols.

3 S.R. and O. 1945. No. 152 (Central Advisory Councils for Education Regulations, 1945) allowed for members to be appointed for six years and Chairmen for three years. This was amended to allow for three-year appointments in S.I., 1951, No. 1742.

4 Education Act, 1944. Section 4 (3).

5 15 to 18'. Report of the CAC (England), HMSO. Vol. 1 Report, Chapter 21, 1959. To be fair, the chapter says it 'deliberately attempts to sketch the Sixth Form at its best'. But all CAC Reports have described the best.

6 See Note 2.

7 See Note 2, particularly Chs. 15 and 16, Plowden Report.

8 See Note 2.

9 See Note 2, Ch. 6.

10 A. Crosland, *The Conservative Enemy*, 1962, Jonathan Cape.

11 E. Boyle, A. Crosland and M. Kogan. *The Politics of Education*, Penguin, 1971, p. 174.

12 A. H. Halsey, J. Floud and C. Arnold Anderson, *Education, Economy and Society: a Reader in the Sociology of Education*, The Free Press, 1961, Intro.

13 Education Act, 1944, Ch. 5, para. 151.

14 See particularly R. M. Titmuss, *Commitment to Welfare*, Allen & Unwin, 1967, Part III.

15 The National Association of Schoolmasters, 'Primary Education', Memorandum submitted to the Central Advisory Board for Education, 1964, p. 5.

16 Hansard, 24 July 1963, and Address to Annual Conference of the Association of Education Committees in *Education* 19 July 1963, pp. 98–106.

17 J. W. B. Douglas, *The Home and The School*, MacGibbon & Kee, 1964.

18 B. Bernstein, particularly 'Social Class and Linguistic Development' in A. H. Halsey (ed.) *Education, Economy and Society*, The Free Press, 1961.

19 For example, J. Floud, A. H. Halsey, F. M. Martin *Social Class and Educational Opportunity*, Heinemann, 1956.

20 Boyle et al., op. cit., p. 173.

21 Hansard, 16 March 1967.

22 Boyle et al., op. cit., p. 25–34.

23 Ibid. p. 174.

24 F. M. White, 'Three Years' Hard Labour – or Life on the Plowden Committee', *Preparatory Schools' Review*, June, 1967.

25 R. S. Peters (ed.), *Perspectives on Plowden*, Routledge & Kegan Paul, 1969.

26 See Note 2, Vol. 1, Paras. 780 to 788.

27 E. Fraser, *Home Environment and the School*, University of London Press 1959.

28 Floud et al., op. cit.

29 Report of the Committee on Local Authority and Allied Personal Socia Services, HMSO, 1968.

30 Local Authorities Social Services Act, 1970.

31 Douglas, op. cit.

32 These were listed in Ch. 30 of Vol. 1.

33 Bernstein, op. cit.

34 Peters, op. cit.

35 *School Government Chronicle* February, 1967. Leading article.
36 Boyle et al., p. 197.
37 Joseph Featherstone, 'The Primary School Revolution in Britain', *New Republic*, 1968.
38 M. Kogan 'The British Primary School: a Model of Institutional Innovation', Educational Planning in Perspective, *Futures* IPC, 1971.
39 These are described in several DES papers in the Second Report from the Expenditure Committee. (Education and Arts Sub-Committee), Session 1970–71.
40 Boyle et al., pp. 173 to 174.
41 Ibid., pp. 132 to 133.

5 The Redcliffe-Maud Royal Commission on Local Government

JEFFREY STANYER

Like many other recent commissions and committees of inquiry the Royal Commission on Local Government in England, 1966–69 (Chairman, Sir John Maud, later Lord Redcliffe-Maud), was concerned with a subject which over the years has become almost entirely the province of applied social science. The analysis of any local government structure is now a set of technical operations in social geography, applied economics and political science. One of the main interests of the work of the Redcliffe-Maud Royal Commission for the student of the processes of modern government is, therefore, the question of whether the Government, if they wish to use the results of social science research, should receive advice based on them through the medium of a largely amateur committee. An evaluation of the Redcliffe-Maud Commission is directly relevant to this question.

GENERAL BACKGROUND

In its historical context, the Redcliffe-Maud Commission appears to be only one phase of a long process, which began after the First World War. This process has been characterised by a series of official investigations which have sought to find a generally acceptable territorial pattern of local authorities as an alternative to the traditional one established between 1888 and 1899.[1] The appointment of these committees and commissions has often been greeted with an enthusiasm for the changes that they may create. Generally this hope has been unfulfilled; though some of them have had a limited success, others have been failures, in that they have not been able to solve the problems that faced them. Their proposals have not usually been implemented.

The most important consequence of this historical context for the Redcliffe-Maud Commission was that its work took place against a background of widely canvassed ideas. As one piece of reforming machinery has replaced another certain general ideas and themes have reoccurred repeatedly, often achieving the status of conventional wisdom. These general ideas, which are largely critical of the present territorial pattern, and the proposed new systems based on them, provide the most important part of the background of the Commission.

By 1966 certain judgements had become widely accepted as the starting point for any proper reform of local government.[2] It was usually argued:

(a) That there are too many small authorities in each legal category of authority.

(b) That the boundaries of local authorities have not changed radically for many years whilst the pattern of everyday life has so greatly altered that the former bear little relation to the latter.

(c) That the existence of different *types* of authority promotes conflict between authorities and makes local agreement on reform in any respect difficult.

(d) That the division of authority within the administrative county creates friction and prevents coordination of related activities.

The state of affairs supposedly revealed by these criticisms was thought to have consequences for both the system of government and the citizen. The central government was forced to take away services from local authorities and made reluctant to allocate new ones. It was also reluctant to trust local authorities to dispose of their duties properly and therefore increased the powers of central control. The citizen was subject to varying standards of service, harmed by the inabilities of local authorities to deal with urgent problems and unable to understand the system in operation.

There was good reason long before the appointment of the Redcliffe-Maud Commission to think that many of these points in the conventional wisdom were fictitious – that is, the alleged 'facts' were not correct and the pattern of authorities did not have the consequences ascribed to it.

It is not surprising that academic social scientists had become interested in the problems implicit in this conventional wisdom but much of the relevant work, in economics and geography as well as political science, had been published in learned journals which are not generally well known to politicians and senior administrators. The significance of the Redcliffe-Maud Commission is that the research that it generated was a turning-point in the discussion of the territorial pattern of local authorities. It brought the results of modern social science to general public attention.

There is, however, one fundamental problem in that the more useful and advanced the social science research is, the more difficult it is for non-professionals to understand it. In fact it is one of the striking features of the Redcliffe-Maud Commission itself that it did not draw the obvious conclusions from the evidence presented to it, but continued to repeat what by 1969 had become discredited clichés.

This is one of the crucial points in understanding the reactions of the public and interested parties to the Commission's proposals. Many of the critics of the Redcliffe-Maud Commission seized on the evidence which throws great doubt on the whole line of reasoning that the Commission employed and thus on the conventional wisdom. The Redcliffe-Maud Commission's work contained some of the causes of its own defeat.

IMMEDIATE BACKGROUND

There was a more immediate reason for the appointment of the Redcliffe-Maud Commission. By late 1965 it was quite clear that the process of reform under the Local Government Act, 1958, was running into difficulties. This Act drew two distinctions which were of importance to the terms of reference of the Redcliffe-Maud Commission. It distinguished between London and the rest of England and between England and Wales. Greater London was excluded from the scope of Part II of this Act and investigated by a Royal Commission, and a separate Local Government Commission was created for Wales.

The differential treatment of England and Wales which began in 1958 was continued as a result of later developments. The Local Government Commission for Wales (1958–63) found that its Report and Final Proposals were completely inacceptable to the Government of the day and new machinery was devised. In 1966 this was believed to be about to produce new proposals and it was thought best not to disturb its work.

The work of the English Commission did result in some changes but as time went on the process became slower and slower and the impact of the limitations in the terms of reference on what could be proposed by the Commission became more and more apparent. The progress of the Commission was such that the Government was faced with the prospect of some areas having had their local government structure completely recast while others had scarcely started on a consideration of change.

A contrast to the fragmentary and lengthy procedures of the Local Government Act, 1958, was to be found in the speed and effectiveness of the Herbert Commission. It had originally been proposed to deal with London at the same time as the rest of England and Wales, but a decision was taken later by the Conservative Government to exclude Greater London from the jurisdiction of the English Commission and was in fact given its own Royal Commission. This Commission sat from 1957 to 1960 and its Report was implemented very largely in the London Government Act, 1963. Not all aspects of the Report were accepted and it generated considerable controversy, but the Government generally adopted the lines of its analysis and carried it through in face of a strong opposition. The system created by the 1963 Act came into full operation in 1965 and there was every reason to think that it would be successful. The traditional advisory procedure of the Royal Commission thus compared very favourably with the new procedure specially devised in 1958 for local government structure.[3]

THE SETTING UP OF THE ROYAL COMMISSION

It is not surprising that in 1965 the Government was obviously considering a new way of dealing with the problems of local government structure and Mr Crossman, the Minister of Housing and Local Government, in a speech at the Association of Municipal Corporations' (AMC) Conference in Torquay on 22 September ranged widely over topics affecting the public image of local government.[4] He frankly admitted the defects of the existing system and canvassed alternatives. One of these was the idea of a small committee acting quickly to establish the fundamental principles on which reform should be based. It was not however until February, 1966, that the Prime Minister himself announced that a Royal Commission rather than the committee envisaged by Mr Crossman was to be created and it was not until some time after that the Chairman and the members were announced.[5]

A POSITIVE OR NEGATIVE INSTRUMENT OF GOVERNMENT

Observers are always concerned with the motives of a Government when it appoints a committee of inquiry. In particular, does it genuinely hope that the Commission will expedite change and improve public policy decisions? Or is it a device for avoiding decisions which would be politically difficult or unrewarding whichever way they were taken? It is of course formally very difficult to distinguish these two cases and for some purposes the distinction is irrelevant.

Probably the Redcliffe-Maud Commission should be viewed originally as a positive instrument of government – that Mr Crossman, the Government and the civil servants behind its appointment thought of it as a way of solving serious problems very quickly. But it seems clear after the first statement by Mr Crossman that the elements of negativism began to dominate.

There is considerable direct and indirect evidence that the civil service is very serious about local government reform. The direct evidence lies in the submissions made to the Royal Commission and to other relevant bodies. The indirect evidence lies in the fact that for several years different ministers and different governments have persevered with the cause of reform, even though it is unpopular and politically difficult, and even though there is little worthwhile evidence that any tangible benefits will accrue to the British people. One may expect governments to attempt politically difficult changes if there are strong reasons to believe that these have considerable benefits generally for the citizens, but not to try dangerous and probably unrewarding ones.[6]

It is easy to see why the elements of negativism should soon become apparent. In the case of local government reform there is only a limited number of proposals that can be made, and each of these has certain consequences for the positions of existing groups and institutions. The local government world is divided into a number of distinct interests and most of these are expressed in organisational terms. As the members of these organisations are generally educated and knowledgeable people, who have considerable time to deal with the political and administrative matters which affect them, they are able to present their cases at length and with skill.

Nor is there any reason why they should accept the word of the Government and the civil service if it points towards a course of action which harms their interests as they perceive them. In the provision of public services the question of responsibility for any alleged defects may be hotly debated. Local authorities are as able to blame the centre for 'failures' in housing, education, police etc. as the centre is to blame local government.[7] Thus the chairman, the composition of the commission, and its terms of reference in detail are very important. Interested groups are rightly concerned with the finer details of the creation of a committee of inquiry as these may effect the way the task is performed and the proposals that emerge from the committee.

The effects of the influence of a disparate group of interested parties may well be to turn what the Government intended as a positive move into a negative one. Established bodies do not mind rapid decision-making if it is in their interest but what they worry about is the speedy and damaging decision.[8]

EVALUATING ADVISORY PROCEDURE – THE APPROACH OF THIS ESSAY

To a large extent speculation about the motives of those acting behind closed doors is irrelevant to the approach adopted here. The Redcliffe-

Maud Commission is to be evaluated in terms of a framework derived from an acceptance of the literal meaning of what is said about it. This framework in fact embodies a naïve approach to the work and report of an advisory committee. The appointment of a Royal Commission or similar body holds out to the citizenry at large and to those specially affected by the subject under investigation the prospect of a greater degree of reasonableness in the ultimate decision, and a guarantee that their perceptions and interests will be properly considered. It is true that this may be a deception but the Commission itself cannot take this view nor ought those who evaluate it in formal terms. It is not foolish to ask how far these formal promises have been fulfilled.

One of the most important facts to grasp about the role of Royal Commissions and Committees of Inquiry is that they are only one part of the whole process of decision-making in government. Decisions are formally the responsibility of the Government and nowhere is this more clear than in the question of the decisions relating to the structure of local government. Governments cannot avoid taking these decisions – they cannot pass them over to other bodies. Nevertheless at the formal level they may well wish to take advice from some sort of authoritative body. But they will not of course be necessarily bound by this advice.

The difference between deciding and advising is sometimes forgotten in this context and commentators often appear to think that a Royal Commission's Report settles a matter. Commissions themselves often forget this distinction and act as though they were determining matters. But behaviour appropriate to a decision maker is not always appropriate to an advisory body.[9]

The actual task of any individual committee or commission of inquiry will be set out in its terms of reference and committees may well differ very much in the role that they have to play, but it is not hard to see that most of them are enjoined to create or discover a set of principles to guide action in the particular field and to produce a set of proposals which are in some sense entailed by these principles. At least, a convincing, plausible and well-executed response to the problems in terms of reference will involve these points.[10]

This approach implies a certain view of the nature of advice giving. Commissions are set a problem or group of problems and are expected to work out the answers in a justifiable manner. Decision-making requires both *a set of values* and a *correct knowledge of how the world works*. As advisory bodies have a special role to play, they stand in a different relationship to the problem of knowledge than to the problem of values.

The relevant knowledge, both factual and contextual, is determined by the logic of the problems and should determine the type of evidence collected and the way it is used. Thus 'evidence' should be relevant, contextually justified, correct, complete and properly employed. This creates one set of evaluative criteria – those relating to the collection and use of evidence.

It also implies that if the Commission makes some new proposals, then these must also be researched – that is, evidence directly relevant to these, comparable to the evidence relevant to the old system, must be gathered and explained.

The problem of values is quite different. Because commissions are part of an advisory process their values are determined by others not by their membership. A commission may make either of two mistakes – it may add further values of its own – which is impertinence – or it may ignore one or more of the given ones – which is dereliction. Additional values can only be introduced if they are intermediate or instrumental values – and this should be shown, otherwise there is the danger of the displacement of the primary ones by those of the individual committee members.

The ease with which a commission can go about its work will be influenced by the characteristics of the values presented to it – their number, their relationship to each other and the preciseness with which they are stated.

In effect what is required in local government reform is the discovery of a set of principles. A principle as defined below joins together facts and values and provides a means of dealing with a variety of disparate situations and circumstances – both aspects of local government reform.

A principle may be defined as a rule of general applicability which, if followed, offers some guarantee that certain values will be promoted. The characteristics of a principle therefore are (a) that it is an imperative, (b) that it has considerable generality, that is, it applies to a wide range of circumstances, (c) that the 'facts' and empirical relationships presupposed by it are correct, and (d) that the previously articulated values are in fact promoted by following the prescribed behaviour. If this is accepted as a proper definition in this context, then it provides a suitable framework in which to evaluate the work of the Redcliffe-Maud Commission.

THE MEMBERS OF THE COMMISSION

Brief biographies of the members of the Commission were given in the *Municipal Review*, July 1969. These show that many members already had definite connections with the local government system – and often were partisans in the proper meaning of this term – that is, closely connected with, or committed to, an interest or organised group. There were only two members who could be said to be neutral in local government terms. The vice-chairman, John Bolton, and Vic Feather, then Acting General Secretary of the TUC, had no previous commitment or contact with local government. The remainder had some specific partisan connection with the local government world. Five members had been or still were council members, whilst two were officers or former officers. One officer and one council member had a county council background whilst the other five were county borough men. From the party-political point of view, if one includes Feather, there were three known Labour party members and two Conservatives. (The partisan affiliations of most members are of course unknown). Occupationally the upper middle class was predominant – two former permanent secretaries of central ministries, a solicitor, several businessmen, two senior local government officers as well as the two in managerial positions in left-wing organisations. There was also a noticeable academic flavour in that three held or had held University posts. Five members had also been on the Committee on Management of Local Government (1964–67).

Dame Evelyn Sharp and Derek Senior have not been included in the neutrals because, although they do not fit into any of the above partisan categories nevertheless their previous deep involvement, of different kinds, with local government makes it impossible to classify them with Feather and Bolton.

A different sort of partisanship was involved in the public commitment of some of the members to particular analyses and proposals in print prior to the formation of the Commission. The most serious example of this arose from the inclusion of Derek Senior in its membership. Senior had been an analyst of local government affairs for a considerable time and had publicly committed himself to a particular line of reasoning. In fact he could easily have gone to the first meeting of the Commission and simply handed round offprints of his 1965 article in *The Political Quarterly*. But the members of the Maud Committee could have presented a collation from their previous Report[11] and several members had written or lectured on local government, at least touching in passing on 'what is wrong'.

THE TERMS OF REFERENCE

The terms of reference were: 'to consider the structure of Local Government in England, outside Greater London, in relation to its existing functions; and to make recommendations for authorities and boundaries, and for functions and their division, having regard to the size and character of areas in which these can be most effectively exercised and the need to sustain a viable system of local democracy; and to report'. The exclusions of Greater London and Wales have already been explained, but there are other features worthy of comment.

First, the consideration was limited to *structure*; the whole of the local government system was not included. In such circumstances it is of course always possible to argue that other factors are implied, but this can be a dangerous procedure. The marginal matters may take up too much time or may be treated in a cursory way. Also in these investigations one is always in danger of being overwhelmed with information – a risk which, it may be argued, severely affected the Redcliffe-Maud Commission.[12]

Secondly, consideration was restricted to existing local government services. No general consideration of the allocation of public services *between* types of local administrative body was possible, though the opinion of many prior to the appointment of the Commission was that the range of local government services should be revised as part of a review of structure. In fact quite the opposite happened as the Government investigated and made proposals for individual services in apparent isolation from the work of the Commission.[13]

Thirdly, no restrictions on what might be proposed were contained in the terms of reference. In previous attempts, restrictions had been written into the operation from the start. The Local Government Boundary Commission could not deal with services as opposed to boundaries, it could not propose county-boroughs in Middlesex nor touch the status of non-county-boroughs. It and the Local Government Commissions were limited by forced assumptions as to minimum sizes of authority. These and other restrictions had rightly incurred the wrath of the commentators and in this respect the Commission was given a free hand.[14]

Fourthly, two types of criterion were provided. The size and character of areas were to be determined by reference to the effectiveness of service provision and to viability of a system of local democracy. These two sets of values have occurred in all the post-war discussions and terms of reference of commissions. But the unfortunate history of 'effective and convenient local government' in the period did not inspire confidence in those who had examined in detail the reasoning previously employed in this context.[15] Thus the values which provide the only possible foundation for the analysis of the problems are presented in vague terms. At least some of the blame for what followed must be attributed to those who conceived and drafted the terms of reference.

HOW THE COMMISSION WENT ABOUT ITS WORK

There were a number of special features about the way this Royal Commission on Local Government operated. Obviously it was given the usual power to call and examine witnesses and papers and was given the usual sort of secretarial assistance. The civil service departments and the local authority associations were specifically asked for written evidence as were the Greater London Council (GLC) and the London Boroughs' Association (LBA). An open public invitation to submit evidence was issued through the press and all individual local authorities were notified of this, as were the National and Local Government Officers Association (NALGO) and the Association of Education Committees (AEC). This produced a total of 2,156 witnesses. Later the views of a number of people were sought informally on particular questions.

As governmental inquiries increasingly today deal with topics that are also the subject of social science research, they have increasingly come to rely on the aid of academics. The Redcliffe-Maud Commission differed from previous investigations of local government structure in this respect. First, it appointed a part-time director of research, and also employed research officers from other government departments. Mr L. J. Sharpe was appointed Director of Intelligence, with the status of Assistant Commissioner, to organise the research programme. He was a Fellow of Nuffield College, Oxford, and had specialised in research into aspects of local democracy. Dr S. W. E. Vince and his team of experts in planning, social geography and map-making helped with the assessment of the mass of information available about economic, social and geographical conditions in the different parts of the country.

Secondly, it commissioned individuals and bodies throughout the country to undertake particular research projects. Eventually ten research studies were available for the Royal Commission; these varied tremendously in scope and intellectual difficulty. The total cost of the research studies is not given in the Report but it must have been considerable.

Thirdly, it published the evidence given to it as it was received, as an alternative to either keeping it secret, allowing individuals to publish their own evidence, or else publishing it after the Committee had reported. It also published the minutes of the verbal evidence. Some documents it was thought unnecessary to reproduce but the major part of the evidence collected was available before the Commission reported.[16]

Thus before reaching its final decisions the Commission had available to it the following 'evidence':

1 The work done by the Local Government Commission for England, the Maud & Mallaby Committees, and the Seebohm Committee (this material was unpublished).

2 Written evidence from:
   (a) 10 government departments (362 pp. + 37 pp.)
   (b)   5 local authority associations (315 pp.)
   (c) 39 county councils (351 pp.)
   (d) 50 county borough councils (183 pp.)
   (e) 116 non-county borough councils (342 pp.)
   (f) 247 urban district councils (717 pp.)
   (g) 215 rural district councils (534 pp.)
   (h) 594 parishes of which 86 were resolutions of a PM (496 pp.)
   (i)   8 bodies in London Government (379 pp. + 2 pp.)
   (j) 50 local government and associated bodies (308 pp.)
   (k) 71 professional organisations (352 pp.)
   (l) 85 commercial, industrial & political organisations (230 pp.)
   (m) 534 private individuals (303 pp.)
   (n) 130 amenity, ratepayers' and residents' organisations and other witnesses (311 pp.)

3 Oral evidence from:
   (a)   6 government departments
   (b)   5 local authority associations
   (c)   the AEC & NALGO

4 Ten specially commissioned research studies by outsiders (1,578 pp.).

5 Ten specially prepared research studies by the Commission's own staff and one each by the Department of Education and Science, and the Home Office. (These twelve were published together as Volume 3 (245 pp.).

The total number of pages of 'evidence' that the members of the Commission were required to read was considerably in excess of 6,745 – the pages of published evidence which do not include the unpublished work or the minutes of oral evidence.

THE REPORT ITSELF

The Report itself consists of fifteen chapters, a summary list of proposals (in the usual manner of Royal Commissions) and nine annexes which present descriptive material relating to both existing and proposed systems. There are also six maps provided in the text and six maps in a folder.

Chapters one and two are not part of the main argument; the first chapter is in effect a summary of most of the whole Report (in six pages) and the second sets out the temporal pattern of the Commission's procedure. The last chapter (Chapter 15) is a short summary of the gains the new system is claimed to have over the existing one.

The main argument is presented in Chapters three to seven. In Chapters eight to ten the details are spelled out for each of the three proposed levels of authority and some extra matters (elections, management and internal organisation, and finance) are considered before a brief guide is given to how the transition to the new structure should be made.

The relative importance of the various topics may be judged by the number of pages devoted to them (note: some of the chapter titles are mine). Thus:

I	Summary	6
II	Procedure	2
III	Need for change	$22\frac{1}{2}$
IV	Insiders' evidence	15
V	Outsiders' evidence	$16\frac{1}{2}$
VI	Principles	10
VII	Application	6
VIII	Main Authorities	12
IX	Local Councils	$13\frac{1}{2}$
X	Provinces	$8\frac{1}{2}$
XI	Elections	$4\frac{1}{2}$
XII	Management	6
XIII	Finance	9
XIV	Transition	$3\frac{1}{2}$
XV	The future	4

Annexes		
1	Description of new units	141
2–7	Further information on existing and proposed systems	24
8–9	Witnesses and research studies	26

One odd point about the Redcliffe-Maud Commission is that it produced three versions of the Majority Report. Most of Volume I is the basic work, but Chapter one (Main Conclusions and How they were Reached) is a six-page version of the rest of the Report and there is also a separate pamphlet, 'Local Government Reform' (Cmnd. 4039), which presents a different summary of the basic work in seventeen pages (with a two-page summary by Senior of his dissent).

The interesting point is that though these three versions of the Commission's ideas are not literally inconsistent, they do in fact give quite different impressions. In fact the short versions are more confident and more dogmatic and give a sense of greater reasonableness than does the bulk of the main Report itself. It is a matter of interesting speculation how far people have read the main work rather than the short versions, as this could be important in understanding their reactions to the specific proposals.

In what follows, the ideas and quotations are drawn from the main part of Volume 1 of the Report. This volume was written by ten of the eleven members as one, Derek Senior, dissented so strongly from his colleagues that he preferred to write his own Report (published as Volume II).

THE NEED FOR CHANGE

The Commission began by arguing that the purposes for which local government existed were not being properly fulfilled under the present structure. They state: 'We conclude then that the purpose of local government is to provide a democratic means both of focusing national attention on local problems affecting the safety, health and well-being of the people, and of discharging, in relation to these things, all the responsibilities of government which can be discharged at a level below that of the national government' (para. 30). 'We do not think that this purpose is being fully realised today. Partly this is due to the fact that local government is severely handicapped by the structure which it is our function to review. . . . But partly also it is due to the fact that there are strongly centralising influences at work' (para. 31). The two purposes mentioned in para. 30 above occur time and time again in the Report. 'The questions that have dominated all our work are these. What is, and what ought to be, the purpose which local government serves; and what, at the present day, is its scope?' (para. 27). 'Our terms of reference also require us to bear in mind the need to sustain a viable system of local democracy: that is, a system under which government by the people is a reality. This we take to be of importance at least equal to the importance of securing efficiency in the provision of services. Local government is not to be seen merely as a provider of services' (para 28).

The demand for centralisation is created by powerful forces in British society – the revolution in communications (para. 32), economic and military considerations and social equality (para. 33), but it is encouraged by the structural weaknesses of local government. These weaknesses will become more striking because of the 'challenges of the future' (pp. 13–21) in the services for which local authorities are responsible.

The main weaknesses identified were:

(a) The division of town and country, embodied in the county/ county borough dichotomy. They say: 'Local government areas no longer correspond to the pattern of life and work in England. Population has long since over-run many of the old boundaries'. (para. 85) . . . 'The failure to recognise [The interdependence of town and country] is the most fatal defect in the present structure. Town and country have always been, and must be, interdependent' (paras 85 and 86) . . . 'The division between county boroughs and counties meanwhile builds into the system a division of interest where, in fact, there is a common interest' (para. 88).

(b) The division of responsibilities within the administrative county: 'Within the counties, the division of responsibility between county and district councils is a great weakness' (para. 89). 'It is not only the physical manifestations of divided responsibility that are wrong under the present system in the counties. It is also the attitudes which the division necessarily engenders. No single authority is responsible for thinking about the totality of related services and their adequacy for local needs; no single authority is responsible for considering the community as a whole' (para. 92).

(c) Small authorities in each legal category: 'Perhaps the most frequently voiced criticism of the present structure is that many local authorities, whether county, county borough or county district councils, are too small in terms of area, population and resources, including highly qualified manpower and technical equipment' (para. 93). 'We find that the minimum size for all the main services is, desirably, a population of some 250,000. If this is compared with the tables of populations set out in Annex 4, it will be seen that 9 out of the 45 counties, 65 out of the 79 county boroughs, and all the county districts, at present fall below it' (para. 94).

(d) The relationship between local authorities and their citizens: 'The relationship between local authorities and the public is not satisfactory. The Committee on the Management of Local Government found that there is both ignorance of and indifference to local government on the part of the public; and indeed it is not uncommon to hear contempt expressed' (para. 95) . . . 'We think that the public's attitude to local government is largely due to the defects in the structure we have outlined. Local government is, at present, apt to be irrelevant to people's problems and often cannot solve them even though it has the responsibility for doing so' (paras 95 and 96).

Their conclusion is therefore: 'In short, what is needed is a clarification of the local government system. The system itself is hard enough for most people to understand, with county borough councils in some of the towns, county and county district councils elsewhere, and very little sense in the boundaries between the two. England needs a pattern of local authorities with clear responsibilities, big enough in area, population and resources to provide first-class services, able to give decisions (subject to whatever control by central government is necessary), and determined to ensure that all their citizens have a reasonably convenient point of access where they can get answers to their questions and advice on how to get whatever help they need. We believe that the public would then become both more aware of local government and more interested in it' (para. 99). If this is done then perhaps a new relationship between central and local government can emerge (pp. 30–32).

To a large extent the above analysis is a highly conventional one and is not particularly derived from the evidence of witnesses or of the specially commissioned research. The latter two are presented in separate chapters, inappropriately titled 'the changes needed', because in the case of the witnesses most of the 'evidence' is a proposal for change rather than a diagnosis, whilst the evidence of research is largely confined to elucidating factual relationships. It might also be thought that the 'evidence' might have been presented first and the Commission's own conclusions as to the need for change based on the discussion of the evidence.

It might also be thought to be an unnecessary discussion – certainly at such a length. The real problem facing the Commission was not to simply repeat the conventional wisdom but to clarify it where it was vague, reject it where it was wrong and supplement it where it was incomplete.

INSIDERS' EVIDENCE

However the Commission then proceed to the evidence of insiders and as most of the insiders in fact repeated that part of the conventional wisdom which suited them, more space and time are wasted on what was already common 'knowledge'.

As it is, the evidence of witnesses is generally presented in a summary, deadpan manner, with great emphasis on the evidence of large national institutions – the central departments and the local authority associations.

'We have published the whole body of evidence. It shows widespread agreement among witnesses on the need to change the present local government system. As our report cannot refer to all the proposals for change put to us, we concentrate in this chapter on three main themes:

    (i) the strong case that witnesses made for the provision of services by much larger units than most present authorities;

    (ii) the need they saw for the organisation of local government to reflect the links between services and

    (iii) their main proposals for a new structure of local government.

These themes cannot always be kept apart, as sometimes witnesses' views on structure determined their views on the size of units and vice versa. In particular, views on structure were often inseparable from the kind of area that witnesses thought necessary for planning' (para. 109).

Most of the witnesses argued for larger authorities but the exact figures quoted varied tremendously and apparently in direct relationship to the interests of the person or body giving the evidence. There was also a substantial body of opinion for strengthening links between services by giving them to one authority, providing a clear division and by ending delegation.

The witnesses tended to favour one of three main structures:

    (i) 'City regions;

    (ii) A two-tier system with geographical counties singly or in combination at the upper-tier and much enlarged district councils, including what are now county boroughs, at the second tier;

    (iii) Authorities responsible for most of the functions of local government (most-purpose authorities), with provincial authorities above them for functions thought to require very wide areas' (paras 157).

The Commission then described each of these three types of proposal in some detail, relating them to the people who supported them. It ended by pointing out that in some respects the three types were similar (paras 177 and 178).

OUTSIDERS' EVIDENCE

The evidence provided by research was rather different in that it was concerned to elucidate the causal relationships between characteristics of areas of local government and the performance of local authorities in one or more specific service.

The evidence of research was considered under three headings: that relating to the facts of modern social geography; that relating to factors influencing performance of individual services and that relating to attitudes to local government generally (democratic viability).

SOCIAL GEOGRAPHY

Part of the research into the social geography of Britain was undertaken by the Greater London Group and relates only to the South East, the area not previously surveyed by the Local Government Commission for England. The Report says: 'We were impressed by the use of various techniques for establishing coherent socio-geographic entities and were interested by the finding that the commuting catchment area of Greater London is smaller than is sometimes supposed. The Group also concluded that the South East outside London cannot be divided completely into city regions, even if their boundaries are extended as far as is compatible with the concept of the city region.'

For the rest of the country the Commission's own research staff investigated town and country relationships, the characteristics of conurbations and the changing patterns of local government areas. The conclusion was:

'The most important message of all the various socio-geographic studies, including that of the Greater London Group, was that the distinction between town and country, exemplified by the existing boundaries between county boroughs and counties, no longer matches the pattern of life of many of the inhabitants in either type of local government area. Our work under this heading emphasised the growing extent to which work-place and service centre are becoming divorced from homes, and how in this, and in many other ways, areas still separately administered are now linked economically and socially. The degree of linkage varied but it was detected in all types of settlement from great urban concentrations to small market towns. The implications of this trend were unmistakable and had a profound bearing on our conclusions. First, if a new system was to reflect the living patterns of the population, now and in the foreseeable future, it must wherever feasible bring town and country together under one local authority. Secondly, there is a hierarchy of socio-geographic areas, all combining town and country, whose relative size depends on the strength of their urban centres and the range of purposes these serve.

It would, therefore, be necessary to decide, in the light of considerations other than those of social geography, what size and shape of socio-geographic unit would best match the needs of local government' (para. 205).

SIZE AND PERFORMANCE

Most of the research under this heading was undertaken by outside bodies but the Commission's own research staff looked at the relationship between size and certain aspects of staffing. The studies undertaken by outside research bodies were:

(a) Housing, highways and certain personal health services. This was undertaken by the Institute of Social and Economic Research at the University of York and was published as Research Study 3.

(b) Education, by the Local Government Operational Research Unit of the Royal Institute of Public Administration, published as Research Study 4.

(c) Education, health, welfare and the children's services, by Mrs Myra Woolf of the Government Social Survey, published as Research Study 5.

The research embodied in these is basically applied statistics as it relates (by means of the appropriate statistical techniques) measures of the characteristics of areas (including size of population) and measures of performance in service provision.

These studies showed that the effect of size on the performance of services by local authorities was uncertain, to say the least, and probably negligible. Of particular importance was that of Myra Woolf which showed that the influence of other factors on certain services left little room for size to have an effect.

The Commission did however reject the obvious conclusion from this evidence and instead preferred to rely on the subjective impressions of certain government inspectors of education and the children's service. (para. 221).

Two further studies were undertaken by the Institute of Local Government Studies (INLOGOV), one of Birmingham CB and the other of a sample of 32 CBs to see what effect scale had on the internal organisation of authorities. These did not appear, from the way the Commission treated them, to have been very influential in the development of the principles used by the Commission to arrive at its proposed new structure.

DEMOCRATIC VIABILITY

Of their research into democratic viability the Commission says:

'This is the third, final and in many ways most important, aspect of our research programme. Unfortunately, it is also the most ambiguous and the least tangible of all three groups of study into which the programme was divided. We had the great advantage of being able to draw upon the research and the findings of the Management Committee which covered a number of aspects in this field. We were also able to re-analyse some of their survey material and to draw upon the findings of other investigations. Nevertheless, there seemed to be five crucial subjects where existing knowledge was meagre or non-existent and on these we therefore concentrated most of our resources. They are—

   (i) the notion of community in relation to local government;
  (ii) accessibility and responsiveness of local government;
 (iii) decentralised administration;
 (iv) parish government;
  (v) public attitudes to local government, and local leadership' (para. 225).

Each of these is discussed at some length but the comments made on the implications of the research are somewhat disjointed.

After this review of insiders' and outsiders' evidence the Commission were ready to identify the general principles and apply them to the circumstances of different parts of England. However, the previous discussion of the faults and the evidence has made it very obvious what most of the 'principles' will be.

The first principle recognised was that the interdependence of town and country should be embodied in the structure of local government. Secondly, the environmental services should be grouped, as should the personal services. Thirdly, wherever possible all services should be put together as the all-purpose authority is the strongest, but there are areas where a two-tier system is necessary. Fourthly, there should be minimum and maximum sizes of authority, especially for the personal services. The range in fact chosen was between 250,000 and one million population. This was one of the reasons which was used to identify those areas (in fact three of the conurbations) for which two-tier local government was appropriate. Fifthly, existing boundaries should be respected as far as possible.

These principles were used to identify what the Commission calls the operational level of local government, but subsidiary consideration led them to propose two other levels of government in addition – a provincial level and a local level. The provincial level would have broad strategy functions and the local level a communal and democratic role. The implications of the principles were summarised as follows:

'The structure of local government would thus consist of
  (i) an operational level for local government services (two-tier in some areas);
  (ii) a more local one to represent communities and
  (iii) a provincial level to set the strategic framework for the operational authorities' (para. 284).

The principles were applied first of all by distinguishing between unitary and metropolitan areas, the latter being suitable for two-tier local government, and then by applying the size range and geographical criteria to the rest of England outside Greater London. The proposals are summarised and compared with the others in Table 1. (p. 126).

Though there are still eight chapters left and long appendices, the main argument is over. Three chapters discuss details of each of three levels of local government, three discuss, in a very unsatisfactory manner, elections, management and finance, and two short concluding chapters bring the Report to an end.

If the Commission correctly identified a set of disparate principles relevant to the reform of local government structure, there still remained the problem of reconciling them where they conflicted. But the Commission nowhere state what weights were to be given to social geography, efficiency, democracy, and the present system. For instance, they recognise that 'the [Greater London] Group's work taken as a whole reinforced us in the conviction that any proposals for a new system must involve striking a balance between the competing claims of various considerations, of which functional and socio-geographic studies, although important, are only some among many' (para. 189). This lack of weighting was a source of great weakness in the credibility of the scheme the Commission proposed.

THE NEW SYSTEM

The proposals made by the majority of the Commission can best be appreciated if they are set out in tabular form and compared with other proposals: this is done in Table 1. The four headings correspond more or less to geographical size of area. The Redcliffe-Maud Commission proposed that England, including London, be divided into eight provinces. Outside Greater London, England should also be divided into sixty-one main authorities. The main authorities were of two types – three of them corresponding to three of the conurbations, were called

metropolitan areas' and these were to have a two-tier system of government – an upper-tier council for the whole of the metropolitan area and
a number of district councils with jurisdiction over part of the area. In
the rest of the country there were to be fifty-eight so-called unitary
authorities responsible for the main local government services. Finally,
at the locality level, existing parish councils, town districts and county
boroughs were to remain as local councils with powers approximately
corresponding to those of the present parish.

The basic division of services was as follows. The province was to be
responsible for provincial strategy, broad planning functions, consideration of local and structure plans etc., plans for recreation, the arts and
tourism, certain types of development, aspects of further education and
the personal services, and it was to raise its money by precepting. It
should be noticed, by the way, that most of these are relatively vague
expressions. All the statutory local government services were to be the
responsibility of the main authorities in the main areas – which meant
the unitary authority in the fifty-eight unitary areas and were to be
divided between the metropolitan council and the metropolitan district
council in metropolitan areas. Local councils were envisaged as consultative bodies, pressure groups acting on behalf of their locality and
the providers of amenities and improvements on a voluntary basis. But
the Redcliffe-Maud Commission also envisaged that local councils
could play a part in the provision of main services where relevant by
delegation from the unitary authority.

The division of the statutory local government services in metropolitan areas between upper and lower tiers was more complicated and
has been set out in Table 2.

THE IMPACT OF THE COMMISSION'S REPORT

It is easy to show that no commission can expect a unanimous acceptance
of proposals for there are always aspects of its work about which people
may legitimately disagree. However well it collects evidence and however logically it marshalls it; however exactly it relates it to the values
prescribed for it, it only needs a person to place a different relative
weight on the separate values to overturn (for that person) the whole
of the analysis. Secondly, there are a number of aspects on which the
evidence will be less than perfect and this leaves scope for personal
judgement. Thirdly, the sort of values to be promoted by the proposed
reforms are usually of a considerable degree of vagueness; people may
therefore legitimately disagree over the meaning of the statements of
purpose. In fact the method of composition of commissions is likely to
introduce these sources of disagreement into their own deliberations.

TABLE 1
Geographical Area

Source	Province	Region	District	Locality
The Majority of the Redcliffe–Maud Commission	8	58 unitary authorities ↖ 61 main authorities ↗ 3 metropolitan areas	none 20 metropolitan districts	existing PCs, UDs, NCBs, CBs.
Derek Senior	5 Subprovincial alternative (0 12–15 0)	35	144 + 4	common councils where desired
The Labour Government Cmnd. 4276	postponed	51 unitary authorities ↖ 56 main authorities ↗ 5 metropolitan areas	none 28 metropolitan districts	existing PCs, UDs, NCBs, CBs
The Conservative Government Cmnd. 4584	postponed	38 'new' counties ↖ 44 main authorities ↗ 6 metropolitan areas	number not yet decided 34 metropolitan districts	parishes in rural districts?

It appeared that the diagnosis of faults of the present system had been accepted by both Labour and Conservative Parties, but this is to a considerable extent illusory as the diagnosis existed and was widely accepted before the Commission was created. The two Parties, however, differed in their acceptance of the proposals for a new system, Indeed, it might be argued that the only reason why the positive side of the Report was not implemented was that the Labour Party lost the 1970 General Election, for it seemed that the then Government was determined to press on with a scheme for reorganisation which differed from the original majority proposals only in detail. It will be clear from an examination of the Local Government Bill at present going through Parliament that the Commission's proposals have been in the end defeated; the two-tier system which they rejected for most of the country has been adopted for the whole country (and for Wales) and more metropolitan areas created than the Commission recognised.

TABLE 2. THE DIVISION OF SERVICES IN METROPOLITAN AREAS

Metropolitan authority
  (i) Planning
     Building regulations
     Transportation
     Intelligence
  (ii) Housing
     (a) metropolitan housing policy
     (b) building in the interests of the metropolitan area as a whole
     (c) building to ensure fulfilment of planning policies
     (d) policy for selection of tenants
     (e) metropolitan rent policy
  (iii) Water supply
     Main sewerage
     Sewage disposal
     Refuse disposal
     Clean air – metropolitan priorities
  (iv) Museums, galleries; promotion of the arts; entertainment, sports, parks and recreation (in interest of whole metropolitan area)
     Nomination of members to authorities for national parks
  (v) Police
     Fire
     Ambulances

  (vi) Co-ordination of investment in metropolitan area

Metropolitan district councils
  (i) Education
     Libraries
     Youth employment
  (ii) Personal social services
     Personal health services
  (iii) Housing (within framework of metropolitan policy)
     (a) building (except as allocated to metropolitan authority)
     (b) house management
     (c) all other housing powers
  (iv) Local sewers and drains
     Refuse collection
     Clean air – local action and enforcement in accordance with metropolitan priorities
     Coast protection
  (v) Museums, galleries; promotion of the arts; entertainment, sports, parks and recreation (in interest of individual districts)
  (vi) Food and drugs
     Weights and measures
     Consumer protection
     Shops Acts

Licensing of places of public entertainment
Registration of births, deaths and marriages
Registration of electors

(vii) All other local government functions (subject to exceptions – see paragraph 345)
(viii) Rating

AFTER THE REPORT WAS PUBLISHED

The key fact, therefore, in the reception of the Report was that the Labour Government in power accepted the Majority Proposals with very few changes whilst the Conservative Party in opposition eventually came to accept a two-tier system. It is not hard to conclude that this reflects the different impact of civil service opinion as opposed to general public opinion. Local government reform is a difficult subject for both political parties, as whatever is proposed some of their supporters are likely to be adversely affected; as far as one can judge the political parties take their cues in these matters from others.

Most of the central government departments gave evidence to the Commission in its early days and many writers have commented on this evidence. The departments generally came out in favour of a few large authorities for the services for which they were responsible without necessarily implying what should be done for other services. The figures of thirty to forty major authorities appeared regularly in government department evidence, with varying reactions to the possibility of minor authorities. Generally, however, the departments were in favour of keeping major services together. They also stressed the importance of the factor of size in the performance of the services for which they were responsible.

The Commission also gave great weight to what the departments said in the text of the Report, something which will be shown to be unjustified in terms of the intrinsic merit of the evidence. It is not surprising that the civil service appears to have welcomed the proposals for main authorities, and the White Paper published by the Labour Government in February, 1970, is probably a testimony to the influence of the officials in this policy area.

Of course, an opposition is largely immune from this sort of influence but particularly vulnerable to the appeals of large sections of public opinion, general and specialised. Although it is hard to be sure what the general reaction was it seems likely that more were against than for Redcliffe-Maud. Academic and semi-academic opinion published in the local government journals seems to have been generally against it, though on a variety of different grounds. Some picked out its treatment of local democracy as being especially doubtful; others concentrated on the way the economic evidence had been ignored.

Many followed Senior in concentrating on social geography. A selection of academic reactions has been published by Geoffrey Smith under the ironic title of *Redcliffe-Maud's Brave New England*. For the reactions of individual local authorities and citizen groups those interested in local government reform are indebted to the collection of statements published by Barry Rose in *England looks at Maud*.[17]

I have not undertaken a statistical analysis of these quotations (there is no point in doing this) but the general impression given is that a large number of citizens, citizen groups and individual local authorities were strongly opposed to the new scheme. Much of this reaction consisted of special pleading and this is not surprising because much of the evidence of individual authorities was of this nature. One of the points that should not be forgotten is that the proposals amounted to very different things in different parts of the country and their impact was correspondingly different, even though a uniformity of name was maintained by the Commission.

The local authority associations also had mixed reactions but again they had committed themselves very strongly in their evidence to the Commission. The tendency was for the associations to maintain their original positions at first, but as time went on a discernible movement was apparent in favour of the two-tier solution. Most of the authorities in county government came together to produce an alternative scheme in late 1969 for two-tier local government over the whole country, not just in the three conurbations. Although the AMC seemed originally in favour of the Redcliffe-Maud scheme to some extent, eventually the NCBs and small CBs forced a reaction towards a two-tier system in early 1970.

Thus by the time the White Paper was published the Government was opposed by almost all organised opinion in the local government world and academic opposition was perhaps symbolised by the letter to *The Times* in February, 1970, signed by a geographer and four political scientists specialising in local government affairs. At about this time the Conservative Party through Peter Walker, its spokesman on local government matters, was committing itself to a different scheme, which would be fundamentally a two-tier one. This promise has been implemented, though probably not to the liking of the academics mentioned above nor to all the local authorities. At the time of writing a Local Government Bill is passing through Parliamentary processes; when it becomes law, the complete failure of the majority's proposals, although partly a fortuitous event, will have been achieved.

Whether or not it is correct that the difference between the reactions of Labour and Conservatives reflects the relative influence of the civil service and public opinion, if the naïve view of advisory processes is taken, the Report must be examined in the light of its intellectual

I

qualities. It is assumed in this approach that these are important in influencing the acceptability of the proposals.

The failure of the majority to convince Derek Senior that he was wrong in his earlier work was perhaps formally one of the chief reasons for the non-acceptability of the Majority Report; anyone who did not like the proposals could find within the Commission itself some support for their views (the other two dissents were insignificant).

The proposals of Derek Senior, who objected to the whole line of positive reasoning of the Royal Commission (though he accepted much of the diagnosis) were as follows: there were to be five provinces, thirty-five regions, 144 + four districts, and common councils where required. He did also consider what he called the sub-provincial alternative, that is, the provision of *elected* provincial councils rather than appointed ones. If these were actually implemented, a prospect which did not seem very likely to Senior, then the region and the province as he envisaged it would both disappear and be replaced by between twelve to fifteen 'sub-provinces'. As Senior's proposals were fundamentally multi-tier (more so than Redcliffe-Maud's) he also had to face up to the division of services between levels. He allocated to the province long-term strategic planning and the promotion of the province in relation to the centre (in fact an advisory role within central government). The region was to be responsible for the *planning-transportation-development* complex, including water supply, sewerage, refuse disposal, capital investment programming, police, fire and education. The district was to be responsible for personal social and health services, housing management, consumer protection and all functions involving personal contact with the citizen. This left the common council at the locality level with a representational and sounding board function, plus a local amenity function, but with no statutory duties nor any part in them. If the subprovincial alternative were to be adopted then the authority would take the place of the region and also have central government functions delegated to it.

I doubt whether anyone who has read both the Majority Report and Senior's dissent does not appraise the latter as the more coherent, elegantly presented, and less open to powerful criticisms on grounds of logic and fact. Some of Senior's criticisms of the majority's lines of reasoning and details of proposals are quite devastating. It was easy for critics and opponents of the proposed new scheme to take issue with the majority; the material was provided by Senior.

THE REPORT AS A TEXT

A set of proposals for a new system of *anything* is in fact a prediction and predictions fail logically if they contain words such as 'must', 'can', 'might'. Anything which reduces the categorical nature of the statements has no place in recommendations for the future. The only exception is that conditional recommendations are legitimate if ways of fulfilling the conditions are also provided.

There is no space for detailing the textual weaknesses of the Majority Report but the following quotation from the last chapter will illustrate what is meant by the above criticisms: 'But the full benefit will not come automatically from structural change. How far its potential value will be realised must depend on the use made of it in practice by citizens, the councillors whom they elect and the professional staff that councillors appoint. The value we shall get from time and money spent on local government will ultimately still depend on the calibre and humanity of councillors and their staff, on the way they organise their work and on the degree of mutual understanding they achieve between themselves and the communities they serve' (p. 143).

'If the present local government system is drastically reformed, its scope extended to include functions now in the hands of nominated bodies and the grip of central government relaxed, England can become a more efficient, democratic and humane society' (p. 147).

These are not proper arguments; they state that if some changes are made then others may follow. In fact they are not far from a tautology – if people's behaviour changes in certain respects, then they will behave differently. If there are several factors which appear to influence the outcome of some situation, there is always the possibility that one or more of these is negligible or redundant.

THE REPORT AS AN ANALYSIS

If the analysis is so obviously wrong in one or more respects that even a poorly informed layman can see its illogicality, then its chances of implementation are correspondingly reduced. The impact of reports is not often so analysed but it is worth exploring as advisory committees hold out to the citizen the prospect of greater rationality in public decision making.

One way to evaluate a report is to look at it simply as a research document – and appraise it in the light of the usual criteria of analysis – relevance, comprehensiveness, consistency, truth and elegance. Criticisms that were made of the Report often reflected the application of these standards to the diagnosis and prescription, especially in relation to the major themes of the Report.

PRINCIPLES

It has already been remarked that one of the aims of the Commission was to produce a set of principles which would imply a set of proposals for a new territorial pattern of local authorities or show that the existing one was the best that could be achieved. What values were to be promoted by these principles? Does the world work in the way that the principles assume?

At the beginning of the Report (the six-page summary) four values are specified (pp. 1–2), but of these only one, *efficiency*, is directly mentioned in the terms of reference. The others, *adaptability*, *autonomy* and *comprehensibility*, are not directly specified. It is a cardinal point of this analysis that in rational advisory processes values are determined externally to the commission; it is therefore irrelevant, if it is not actually impertinent, for the members of a commission to introduce other values into the analysis. Other values ought therefore to be introduced with great caution; they can only be acceptable if they are instrumental or derived values.

In this case it is not hard to see that two of the values can be derived from the original terms of reference. The latter impose on the Commission the search for an effective exercise of functions in a viable system of local democracy in so far as these can be affected by the territorial pattern of authorities. *Adaptability* means the potential for changing to meet new circumstances so that effectiveness and democracy are maintained. Likewise *comprehensibility* can be regarded as something which contributes both to the effectiveness of service provision and to democracy (the difficulty with this value is not its relevance but its meaning). However, the case is quite different with autonomy. To demand a reduction of central control is irrelevant and introduces an extra value. The Redcliffe-Maud Commission were obsessed with central control; though they recognise the force of the reasons which have brought it about, they really discount them when they come to talk about the new system.

At other places other values are introduced – value for money, general happiness, etc. – and these can usually be represented as derived from the original values. The trouble with some of these is ambiguity. Some extremely important general points may be made about the commission's work deriving from the importance of values.

First, if values are cast in ambiguous or uncertain terms this gives a scope for disagreement simply on verbal grounds. Secondly, if the situation is one of a multiplicity of values then it is necessary to provide some means of relating them when they clash – it is simply not good enough to list the values. Thirdly, if the values are ambiguously stated then it is impossible to provide a means of relating them. In a multi-value situation it becomes more, not less, important to be precise about the meaning of the words which state them. By introducing extra values the Commission make the task harder for themselves.

An example of the problem of ambiguous values arises in the Commission's treatment of comprehensibility. *Comprehensibility* was made one of the central values of the Majority's analysis. However, it is on the point of *comprehensibility* that most criticism was made of the new proposals. A distinction may be made between *general* and *particular* comprehensibility. By the former is understood a knowledge of the way the system works generally without any reference to a particular service, a particular authority or a particular citizen's problems. It is, in fact, academic knowledge rather than practical knowledge. By *particular* comprehensibility is meant a knowledge of the way the individual system works when a citizen has a specific problem – for instance, a mentally retarded child or an aged parent.

There can be no doubt that *particular* comprehensibility is valued by most citizens. When they have a particular problem they want to have an easy and clear way of going about dealing with it – they want to know where to go, who to see, what their rights are, etc. But *general* comprehensibility does not have the same features – it is knowledge which is expensive to acquire, constantly being outdated and to which no use can ever be put. The fact that boundaries in the Greater Manchester area are obscure and outdated is irrelevant to the citizen of Penzance.

At places the Commission seems to treat comprehensibility as a sort of mystical relationship between citizen and government, thus subscribing to the view that general comprehensibility is the important concept. Also if it had stressed particular comprehensibility it would have been concerned with such factors as the location of offices and the length of bureaucratic chains of command.

What is more important is that in operational terms the proposals of the majority would have been much less comprehensible both in general and in particular terms. There are four main reasons for this judgement:

(a) The proposals are for a mixed three- or four-tier system which would be more complicated than the present system in many parts of the country.

(b) Many of the authorities had very curious geographical bases – at least as out of date as the present ones [this is one of Senior's criticisms].

(c) A large part of local government administration would have to be carried out through decentralised machinery and this is *a priori* more difficult to understand than direct administration.

(*d*) Constituencies would be very large in general, thus making dealings with the elected representatives more difficult and more remote.

A criticism made of the present administrative county by the Commission is that it divides responsibility for services which should be joined. But in the metropolitan areas, the Commission itself divides services (see Table 2) and in unitary areas there is the division between the statutory functions on one hand and the broad strategy of the provinces and amenity functions of the localities on the other. Thus the Redcliffe-Maud Commission itself commits exactly the mistakes that it attributes to the present system and fails to follow its own principles.

EVIDENCE

A principle implies a view of the way the world works and it is the function of evidence within the commission's work to provide a defensible view. Evidence ought to be relevant, contextually justified (that is, in the science to which it belongs), factually correct and complete. Each of these has certain implications.

The relevance of the evidence is determined by the values to be promoted. If a value is conceived as a variable, then the evidence should show that the score on this variable achieved by a particular arrangement (of institutions in this case) is higher than on other arrangements (or lower if the variable is a 'bad').

As for contextual justification, this is best approached by considering the difference between insiders' and outsiders' evidence. By 'insiders' is meant the local authority associations, individual local authorities, government departments, professional associations, political parties etc. – all of whom are part of the system or very closely and directly connected with it – in behavioural terms they are participants with vested interests in the present system and possible changes. Outsiders are mainly those who were commissioned to do research on general or particular points, and include the Commission's own research staff. What they have in common is that the collection and presentation of evidence is done by the exercise of a particular academic expertise.

The difference in standing between the two is reflected in the distinction between the intrinsic and extrinsic justification of evidence. These adjectives refer to a relationship between the reasons given and the conclusions. The evidence of insiders is held to be justified in terms of the status of those giving evidence – that is, externally to the evidence itself. An intrinsic justification is one solely in terms of the features of the evidence itself not in terms of the standing or position of those giving it.

The trouble with the extrinsic justification of evidence is that it leads to all sorts of difficulties. First, it can be used either way; one can sometimes say that the evidence given by interested parties is discredited for that reason alone – but on others it can be regarded as justified for that reason alone. Special inside knowledge may be regarded as either virtuous or contaminated.

One of the main problems arises when the evidence conflicts. This is not a problem in intrinsically justified evidence because the conflict is resolved by the relevant intellectual processes, but this cannot happen if it is extrinsically justified. The person judging the evidence is forced to decide in terms of the status of the persons giving the evidence, something which it is very difficult to do in the context of a Royal Commission, though Redcliffe-Maud came very close to it. Once a choice is made between insider 'experts' then the argument becomer one about *bona fides*, motivation and the personal characteristics of witnesses.

The evidence collected by those commissioned to do research is, of course, justified in terms of the academic subject to which it belongs. Outsiders contributed evidence under two headings – the socio-geographical evidence that there are between 130 and 140 distinguishable areas in England outside Greater London, and the exercises in applied economics which related performance to size and other aspects of areas. Each of these has its own internal logic and therefore the conclusions of the studies have to be appraised by the relevant intellectual criteria, that is, intrinsically.

These two types of research relate exactly to the fundamental problems of defining all systems of areas in public administration – not simply of local government. A general review of the principles developed over the years shows that they can easily be divided into two groups – those that relate the pattern of areas to the spatial distribution of living patterns – the community principle – and those that relate them to factors making for the efficient or effective provision of public services. The latter will be treated at length as part of the crucial argument of the central paragraphs of the Majority Report.

 Community has been defined in a number of ways. The simplest way is simply in terms of adjacent settlement patterns; this is a very easy and usable definition of community but perhaps it does not always correspond with people's behaviour. The behavioural community is defined in terms of interaction patterns – including commuting, residential change, recreation, and shopping. Thirdly, there is the subjective community – the community to which people think they belong.

The concepts of both behavioural and subjective spatial community are sophisticated ones, which can only be identified by elaborate and difficult techniques. There is reason to believe that subjective community is in the last analysis not a very helpful concept; methods of studying it tend to run foul of the self-answering question – the community you find is determined by the way you choose the questions put to the respondents. There is good reason to think that the appropriate and usable concept is that of the behavioural community – this is perhaps implicit in what the Commission say about fitting the pattern of areas to the pattern of everyday life.

Derek Senior exploits the fact that size and performance of services are not related, or at least not closely related, to argue that it is better to start from social geography and fit services to these factors rather than adopt a size criterion and then try to manipulate social geography. By doing this, Senior is able to show first that the so-called unitary principle is nonsense in many parts of the country, and secondly that the Majority's treatment of existing boundaries cannot be reconciled with the professed attachment to modernising the structure of local government. The results are nonsensical proposals in many parts of the country.[18]

In perhaps one of the most significant sentences in the whole of the volumes published by Redcliffe-Maud, Senior says (para. 140, vol. 2.) 'My first positive recommendation, then, is that an adequately manned professional team should immediately be set up in the Ministry of Housing and Local Government to produce the background of socio-geographical information that will enable definite boundaries to be rationally drawn when the Government has decided, after the appropriate consultations, what type of new structure to adopt.'

This tells all. The elaborate discussions of areas and the detailed recommendations of the Commission (and by implication of Senior himself) are largely guesses. This is confirmed when one looks in detail at the socio-geographical evidence gathered for Volume III.[19]

OMISSIONS

The most striking omission from the new system was an investigation of political-administrative considerations. It is well known that there are different styles of politics and administration in different parts of the country at the present time. For instance, some authorities are structured in terms of a pattern of area conflicts; others are one-party systems. The way business is disposed of varies from place to place. It may be that these factors are not related to the territorial pattern of local authorities, but this is something that the Redcliffe-Maud Commission was committed to *dis*believing.

Despite the importance of these factors they were ignored with few exceptions in the Commission's research plan. Partly this was because members of the Commission thought they knew the answers to these questions, but also it reflects the general tendency of the Commission to ignore what they themselves said was as important to them as efficiency – namely a viable system of local democracy. But to write about local democracy without considering party systems and administrative politics seems in retrospect incredible. It would not have been very difficult to estimate the sort of party systems likely to be found under various proposed structures, nor to do research into the present relevant authorities to see what patterns of area conflict were likely to emerge.[20]

Another problem of completeness is revealed when a comparison is made of what is known of the existing system with what is known of the proposed system. A lack of evidence about the non-existent one permits its supporters to ascribe any virtues they wish to it but equally it permits its opponents to ascribe any vices they wish. Evidence must be complete in relation to what is proposed. Thus the Commission is under a pressing imperative – it must anticipate and meet criticisms of *its* system as well as refute the defenders of the *status quo*. It must investigate its own proposals to the same degree.

The Commission failed to do this; most of the operational features of the new system are left completely unresearched when a little ingenuity could have provided evidence which might have countered, for instance, the very telling R. E. Mote campaign. For instance, it is obvious that in most parts of the country what the Commission was proposing was government by area administration – the field offices of the unitary authority. This is, however, one of the darkest areas of local government research in the sense that no-one knows anything about it; yet it would have been easy for the Commission to investigate it as already most counties operate by means of identical machinery. Likewise it is not true that in all parts of the country town and country are divided for purposes of major services. Over large parts of the East Midlands town and country are united for planning purposes; this gives a perfect opportunity for looking at the effects of this union compared with other areas in which they are divided – Cambridge might be compared with Oxford, for example.

THE CRUCIAL ARGUMENT

Whatever else may be said of the rest of the Commission's Report, it is clear that the crucial part of the argument occurs in paragraphs 217 to 221 inclusive. They also provide illustrations of some of the main points of this essay.

The tensions that can be produced in a commission are perfectly illustrated by their treatment of the evidence relating to size and performance. The Commission find that the specially commissioned evidence has failed to show that there is a relationship between scale of operation and efficiency in the performance of quite a large range of services. Then they go on to argue that the research on which so much money has been spent must be dismissed as inconclusive for two reasons – (a) that the researchers were only able to study existing systems and there was no guarantee that their conclusions would apply to a totally new system and (b) it is very difficult to find a satisfactory measure of performance in the provision of services (paras. 219 & 220).

Both these statements are of course true. But what makes the Royal Commission's espousal of them a grotesque impertinence is that these are exactly the difficulties detected by the Local Government Operational Research Unit (LGORU). After the LGORU had embarked on its studies for the Royal Commission it decided that the method which had been agreed was subject to grave disadvantages and that a much better model which would overcome the two difficulties mentioned above could easily be devised. The Royal Commission refused to allow the Unit to proceed with the analysis which would have avoided the criticisms levelled in paras. 219 and 220 of the Main Report. (See Research Study No. 4, p. 2 and Appendix 1.)

The paragraph in which the Commission rejects the special studies by outsiders in favour of the evidence of some central civil servants is worth quoting in its entirety:

'For these reasons the two studies by central departments were particularly helpful since they enabled us to supplement what were essentially statistical exercises with the subjective impressions of those who have direct, disinterested knowledge of the quality of local authority performance in two major services. They both showed that size was related to performance. From the returns made by Your Majesty's Inspectorate, the Department of Education and Science concluded that the least efficient education authorities tended to have populations below the 200,000 mark and that authorities above 200,000 but less than 500,000 provided an acceptable or better education service. The best average performance came from authorities with populations above 500,000. The study by the Home Office found a rather less positive correlation between size and efficiency. Nevertheless, the general trends were clear: the most efficient children's service was provided by authorities with populations between 350,000 and 500,000 and those providing the least efficient service tended to have populations below 200,000. (para. 221).

Having rejected the expensively acquired research findings on grounds of logical difficulties which it imposed on them, the Royal Commission then said it found particularly helpful the subjective impressions of Her Majesty's Inspectors of Education and the Children's Service. As one commentator has pointed out, though the Commission say that these supplement the essentially statistical studies, in fact they contradict the outsiders' evidence.[21]

There are so many things wrong with this paragraph. First, it contains some factually wrong statements. HMI's do not have disinterested knowledge of the quality of local authority performance; on the contrary they are leading protagonists in the buck-passing situation mentioned earlier (see p. 109). No correlations are in fact presented in the research studies which report the HMI findings. Secondly, the scoring system used by the HMI is to some extent weighted in favour of large authorities because of the importance it attaches to specialist staff, senior administrative staff and staffing policies in general. (See pp. 332 and 343 of Volume III.) Thirdly, even if the judgements were correct (and there is no evidence to think that they are) in respect of the aspects of the two services chosen, this does not imply that the same relationships would be found in other aspects of the same services or in other services. Fourthly, the evidence of the Inspectorate is subject to exactly the same criticisms and to the same degree that the evidence of outsiders is – it does not apply to a new system nor does it quantify the problems of measurement of quality in a defensible way. To illustrate the point further, consider the following two quotations taken from the revered evidence of the HMI; 'counties . . . tend to show better performance within the same size group than county-boroughs within this size group' (p. 230) and 'It is in the smaller county-boroughs that a concentration of weaker authorities is to be found' (p. 238) and 'Counties provide, on balance, better services than county-boroughs, but the demand for their services may be less intense' (p. 242). Why the Commission did not conclude from this 'evidence' that the two-tier system was better than the unitary system is hard to see.

These three paragraphs raise the whole question of the justification of 'evidence' yet again. It is clear that the intrinsic justification of evidence is quite different from its extrinsic justification. But what if the two clash? If this occurs the only possibility is to reject insiders' evidence and accept the intrinsically justified. Any other course is completely at variance with the promises implicit in the original appointment of a commission. The Royal Commission is this instance was set a task which was nothing more or less than applied social science – it is arrogant for a commission of laymen (basically) to presume to deny the intellectual developments of 100 years in geography and economics.

No-one who has studied the evidence can fail to conclude that the factors affecting the performance of public services in localities are in general not those that can be changed by structural reform; organisational considerations play only a small part in determining the adequacy or otherwise of service provision in a great range of services. If this is so then it might be thought that the community principle should be allowed to play the major role. As has been seen this is very largely what Derek Senior did by making social geography the starting point of his alternative analysis.

CONCLUSION – A WASTE OF PUBLIC MONEY

It was quite clear from the evidence of insiders that no set of proposals would commend wide acceptance; the evidence given by interested parties was such as to make it clear that each was committed to a particular point of view. But in line with an acceptance of the 'naïve' view of the work of commissions, it may be said that although no degree of rigour or factual correctness can guarantee that the opposition will change its mind or melt away, yet a failure to present powerful arguments may generate or increase opposition. A cynic may with reason think that some commissions have been 'anything but action', but the commission itself ought not to take this attitude – or members ought not to accept the appointment if they believe that this is the case.

It may be assumed that generally commissions are not appointed unless the terms of reference contain complicated and difficult problems about which there has been some, if not considerable, controversy over the years. Given these facts no commission can hope to produce a definitive answer; there is no way of destroying or metamorphosing the attitudes of interested parties completely. All that a commission can hope to do is to transform the area of debate and it can only do this by the strength of its arguments, the completeness of the evidence collected and the elegance of its report. The Redcliffe-Maud Commission achieved none of the three aims in its Majority Report and thus it had very little affect on the nature of the debate about local government reform. By producing such a defective text the Commission contained the seeds of its own downfall for its faults enabled its opponents to levy damaging criticisms of its proposals and justify their own attitudes.

Thus at the end of the matter the Redcliffe-Maud Commission must be adjudged a waste of public money. One does not know whom to pity most – all those earnest people and bodies who prepared evidence only for it to receive such summary treatment, or the taxpayer who contributed £379,000. What is most maddening, however, is that it would have been so easy to have made a much better job of the task set.

NOTES

1 The important statutes were:

The Local Government Act, 1888.
The Local Government Act, 1894.
The London Government Act, 1899.

Previous official investigations include:

The Royal Commission on Local Government, 1923–28 (Onslow).
The Local Government Boundary Commission, 1945–49 (Trustram Eve).
The Royal Commission on Local Government in Greater London, 1957–60, (Herbert).
The Local Government Commission for Wales, 1958–63 (Myrrdin-Evans).
The Local Government Commission for England, 1958–65 (Hancock).

Inquiries into individual local government services, such as police, libraries and sewage, are indirectly investigations into local government structure.

2 It should not be assumed at this point that these judgements are either correct or useful. On the contrary it will become apparent later that they all contain difficulties which make their understanding more complicated than is usually assumed.

3 For fuller details of the immediate background to the appointment of the Commission see J. Stanyer, Chapters 1 and 2 in H. V. Wiseman (ed.), *Local Government in England and Wales, 1958–69*, Routledge & Kegan Paul, 1970, pp. 1–41; J. E. Trice, 'Welsh Local Government Reform – An Assessment of Ad-Hoc Administrative Reform', *Public Law*, 1970, pp. 277–296; G. Rhodes and S. K. Ruck, *The Government of Greater London*, Allen & Unwin, 1971.

4 R. H. S. Crossman, 'Basic Reorganisation of Local Government', *Municipal Review*, Vol. 36, No. 431, pp. 655–660.

5 The Prime Minister's announcement was on 10 February 1966, but the Royal Warrant establishing the Commission was not published until 31 May 1966.

6 The evidence for civil service attitudes is most obviously found in the work of the Redcliffe-Maud Commission itself but since 1945 investigations of individual services have revealed the entrenched belief that structure is the basic influence on behaviour in local government. It is now impossible to assent to this general belief, though it may be true in particular spheres.

7 Ioan Bowen Rees founds his rejection of the centrally inspired proposed reforms of Welsh local government on this point. See I. B. Rees, *Government by Community*, Charles Knight, 1971.

8 It is often implied in discussions of local government reform that local authorities should ignore their own beliefs and values by passively accepting the assertions of others. This is not a position that is tenable if it is examined in detail.

9 For instance the decision-maker may wish to take into account special factors which the adviser has been instructed to ignore.

10 Mr Crossman himself had originally made the discovery of *principles* the primary aim of the committee he was considering creating. See *Municipal Review*, Vol. 36, No. 431, p. 660.

11 D. Senior, 'The City Region as an Administrative Unit', *The Political Quarterly*, Vol. 36, No. 1, 1965, pp. 82–91; *The Report of the Committee on the Management of Local Government* (the Maud Committee Report).

12 See p. 115 for an analysis of the amount of 'evidence' presented to the Commission.

13 See the survey of administrative developments by B. C. Smith and J. Stanyer, published annually since 1968 in *Public Administration*.

14 See J. Stanyer in H. V. Wiseman (ed.), op. cit., Chapter 2.

15 See J. Stanyer in H. V. Wiseman (ed.), op. cit., Chapter 2, pp. 25–26.

16 The gross cost of publishing operations was £110,897, of which £17,642 had been recovered in sales when the Report was published.

17 G. Smith (ed.), *Redcliffe-Maud's Brave New England*, Charles Knight, 1969; B. Rose (ed.), *England Looks at Maud*, Justice of the Peace Ltd., 1970.

18 See Volume II (Senior's dissent), pp. 9–19.

19 An analysis of the sort of geographical evidence necessary to define boundaries authoritatively cannot be given here; suffice it to say that if the proper sort of research had been done the Majority would have been in a much better position to argue against their critics, including Senior.

20 Several commentators have made a special point of this omission. See G. W. Jones in G. Smith (ed.), op. cit., pp. 33–36; B. Rose (ed.), op. cit., pp. 158–163.

21 I. B. Rees, op. cit., pp. 21–26.

6 The Seebohm Committee on Personal Social Services

N. M. THOMAS *

'We recommend a new local authority department, providing a community-based and family-oriented service, which will be available to all. This new department will, we believe, reach far beyond the discovery and rescue of social casualties; it will enable the greatest number of individuals to act reciprocally, giving and receiving service for the well-being of the whole community. The new department will have responsibilities going well beyond those of existing local authority departments. . . .'[1]

With these brave words the Seebohm Committee introduced its report. Just twenty-two months later, on the last day of the outgoing Labour Government, the Local Authority Social Services Act, 1970, implemented the Committee's major recommendation. This event must be seen as a major political achievement: it ended several years of agitation which had come to a head during Labour's period of office.

GENERAL BACKGROUND

The development of the personal social services since the Second World War closely parallels the path to the emergence of new professions and semi-professions which H. L. Wilensky,[2] among others, has noted. Along this path the development of a standardised training, the formation of a professional association and the struggle to establish control in the work organisation are inextricably linked.

* I am indebted to many people for their generous help with this study. Lady Serota, Mr Robin Huws Jones and Professor Roy Parker responded to my impertinent questions with great openness. Miss Lucy Faithfull gave freely of her background knowledge of the report and Mrs Pheobe Hall unselfishly shared the results of her own research into a similar topic. The late Sir Charles Barratt's gift of his personal copy of Committee papers to Birmingham University was also invaluable. Mrs Margaret Clarke has worked tirelessly in typing the manuscript.

The major legislative backcloth to these changes was the National Health Service Act, 1946, and the National Assistance and Children Acts of 1948 which had given the local authorities powers and duties to provide health, welfare and children's services. The overriding concern at the time when the legislation was framed was with the provision of residential services for people coming under the care of the local authority – in particular for deprived children, the elderly and the homeless. The role of the social worker hardly existed in these services at that time. Social workers were to be found almost exclusively in the hospitals, the Probation Service, and in voluntary organisations.

Paradoxically the post-war period has been characterised by the growth in community care: a range of services has been established to support people in their own homes or in settings similar to a domestic situation.[3] The Children's service has developed preventive work with families at risk, peripatetic housemothers to look after families during the mother's absence, foster care for children and advice centres to act as a focal point for people needing help. Services for the aged have developed to include home helps, chiropody, meals on wheels, special housing and so on. There have been parallel developments in services for mentally disordered, physically handicapped and (to a limited extent) homeless people.

Many of the legislative changes since 1948 have been designed to catch up with and facilitate progressive professional practice, which had developed beyond existing legal powers and was in danger of being declared 'ultra vires'. Thus the Children and Young Persons' Act, 1963, made provision for preventive work with the families of children 'at risk' of being taken into care, kept in care or taken before a court: the Mental Health Act, 1959, facilitated informal work with patients; and latterly the promotion of the welfare of the elderly was legalised under the Health Services and Public Health Act, 1968.

R. M. Titmuss has noted that 'during the last twenty years, whenever the British people have identified and investigated a social problem, there has followed a national call for more social workers'.[4] Certainly many of the expert inquiries since 1948[5] have borne out Titmuss's statement, whether they were examining services for specific minority groups of people, such as probation and child care, or whether they were looking at broader services, such as hospitals, schools and to a lesser extent, housing departments and general practice. Indeed a greater interest has developed within these major services in the social and emotional aspects of their work. Thus the Royal Commission on Medical Education noted that 'all students should be taught to recognise the effects of their own behaviour upon others' and should develop knowledge of 'the social and cultural factors which influence patients' response'.[6]

A second, equally common, cry has been for proper co-ordination of these and related workers. The initial concern was for co-ordination of services for the neglected child, which in 1950 manifested itself in a joint circular from the Home Office, and the Ministries of Health and Education[7] advocating formal co-ordination arrangements. These calls for co-ordination were extended over time to services for other groups of people. At the same time criticism of the existing arrangements grew and with it the demand for reform of the existing administrative responsibilities. It is notable that all the inquiries referred to above were limited to the work of specific departments or with particular groups of people: none had the opportunity to survey the field as a whole. Divided responsibility for these services at central government level undoubtedly contributed to this separatism. The services did not develop evenly and differences between local authorities in the quality of service remain considerable as Appendix G of the Seebohm Report indicates. The Association of Children's Officers found in 1964 that 90 per cent of child care officers were trained in some authorities whilst other authorities had no trained staff at all.

The growth of training for social workers had not in fact kept pace with the increased demand, partly because the demand was not expressed in terms of marked increases in establishment until the 1960s. The shortage of suitably qualified child care staff was deemed sufficiently serious in 1946 for the Curtis Committee[8] to issue an Interim Report, which led to the establishment of the Central Training Council in Child Care as a non-statutory body in advance of the 1948 Children Act. Yet by 1960 only 681 women and 67 men had been trained as child care officers and many of these had subsequently left the service. Training for fieldworkers in local authority health and welfare departments hardly existed until the 1960s: excluding social workers in child guidance clinics, only 91 social workers out of over 2,000 in health and welfare departments had full professional qualifications in 1957.[9]

The Report of the Younghusband Working Party on Social Workers in Local Authority Health and Welfare Services, 1959, led to the establishment in 1961 of the Council for Training in Social Work and from it the growth of two-year courses for general social workers, largely in the colleges of further education. Similar courses were established by the Central Council for Training in Child Care, which had the advantage of being able to finance courses via its close link with the Home Office. The latter also expanded its traditional interest in University post-graduate courses. A major and continuing expansion of training had begun. The Younghusband Report also resulted in the establishment in 1961 of the National Institute for Social Work Training as a centre for research and post-experience teaching. It had a major role in training social workers to teach on the new courses and, along with the university social work departments, it acted as a focus for social work development.

The Younghusband Report epitomised the growing trend towards the common 'generic' training of social workers, regardless of their particular work setting, which had begun in some of the university postgraduate courses. Such a movement coincided with an increasing recognition among social workers of their common identity, which culminated in the creation of the British Association of Social Workers as a single professional association. Before the Second World War there had been a loose federation of separate social worker associations. This had broken up after the war, leaving a newly created and rather small Association of Social Workers who were committed to eventual unification. This association had set up a working party on registration, from which grew, in 1955, a joint training council of the various social worker organisations. This council in turn developed into the Standing Conference of Organisations of Social Workers in 1963. Finally all but the National Association of Probation Officers were subsumed into the British Association of Social Workers in 1970.

It is important to remember that social workers form only a small minority of employees in the social services departments which the Local Authority Social Services Act brought about. Appendix L of the Seebohm Report shows that in 1966 a total of nearly 90,000 employees would have been included, less than 8,000 of them could be termed social workers and only one in five of these had full professional qualifications.

Julia Parker and Rosalind Allen[10] report a lack of generalised professional goals among social workers working in one county borough in 1965. In addition, the dividing line between social work and many other 'helping occupations' – notably youth and community workers, health visitors and school counsellors – is far from clear.

Nonetheless the most persistent and outspoken critics of the existing administrative arrangements came from leaders of the social work associations or from academics and politicians closely associated with social work.

IMMEDIATE BACKGROUND

Developments in the services for children were the factors which precipitated the appointment of the Seebohm Committee.

There had been increasing pressures for changes in the law so that more help could be given to families containing children who were in danger of being taken into local authority care due to child neglect or who were likely to come before the juvenile counts as delinquent or beyond their parents' control. Similarly, there was pressure to 'remove the stigma of criminality' from children committing offences and to treat them in the same way as other needy children. As a result, the Ingleby Committee[11] was established in 1956 to inquire into the working of the law in England and Wales relating to juvenile courts, remand homes, approved schools and the prevention of cruelty to children and 'to inquire whether local authorities should be given new powers and duties to prevent or forestall the suffering of children through neglect in their own homes'. The Committee was composed mainly of magistrates and lawyers and the bulk of its report, published in 1960, was concerned with detailed changes in juvenile court proceedings. It also proposed increased local authority powers to prevent family break-up, which were embodied in the 1963 Children and Young Persons' Act.

But pressure to enlarge the Children's service into a 'family service' was rejected as 'well outside our terms of reference'.[12] The Committee did, however, urge further consideration of these proposals as a possible long-term solution. In them the prevention of family break-up would have been further emphasised by the provision of marriage guidance, temporary accommodation for unmarried mothers, rest homes for mothers and children and so on. They had been urged most strongly by D. V. Donnison and Mary Stewart[13] in a Fabian Society pamphlet, and by the Council for Children's Welfare and the Fisher Group.[14] The Ingleby Report was roundly condemned by these same people.[15]

The strength of opinion in favour of such administrative reform grew, however, such that in Scotland the McBoyle Committee[16] suggested in 1963 that local authorities should 'set up a family welfare service to make available to the family as a unit the services now provided for individual members of it by separate departments of the local authority'. The Kilbrandon Committee[17] – the Scottish equivalent of the Ingleby Committee – recommended a 'social education department' as an alternative to a family service. This was to include the existing child-care service, the probation service in so far as it dealt with juveniles and the school welfare and attendance service. The reform was to be matched by a new system of juvenile panels, able to treat all children coming before them on the same basis, whether or not they had committed an offence.

In the same year Lord Longford persuaded the Labour Party to set up a study group under his chairmanship, to examine the growing problem of crime. This was an important group because it included several members of the future Labour Government along with a number of outside experts. Social work and the Labour Party thus joined together for the first time since the 'great divide' in the Royal Commission on the Poor Law 1905–09.

Among the group's members were Miss Alice Bacon (later Minister of State at the Home Office), Lord Gardiner (later Lord Chancellor), Mr Elwyn Jones (later Attorney General), Mr Anthony Greenwood (later Colonial Secretary), Miss Margaret Herbison (later Minister of Pensions and National Insurance), Mr James MacColl (later Joint Parliamentary Secretary at the Ministry of Housing & Local Government), Mr Reginald Prentice (later Minister of State at the Department of Education and Science) and Mrs Bee Serota (later a member of the Seebohm Committee). Lord Longford also joined the Cabinet in October 1964 as Lord Privy Seal.

The group, under Lord Longford's prompting, turned itself into a mini-commission, sitting for three months and taking verbal and written evidence from many individuals and organisations.

The starting point of the study was with adult crime, but due to the weight of evidence put to it and to the work of its sub-committee on children and delinquency, it paid considerable attention to the services for juveniles.

Its report[18] contained many far-reaching proposals, including one for the appointment of a high-powered committee of inquiry into the administrative structure of the social services. This was expected to take some time, so that 'as a first step' a Family Service should be established by local authorities to take over the work of existing children's departments and those functions of health, education and welfare departments concerned with family problems. This was to be accompanied by raising of the age of criminal responsibility, so that offenders below school age would be dealt with in civil 'Family Courts' which would also deal with other domestic matters.

When the Labour Government came to power in 1964 Miss Alice Bacon was made responsible Minister of State at the Home Office, with Sir Frank Soskice as Home Secretary. Mr Douglas Houghton, Chancellor of the Duchy of Lancaster, was given responsibility for co-ordinating the social services. Reform along the lines of the study group's proposals seemed imminent and reform of some kind was envisaged in the Queen's speech.

But concern was growing that the mooted reforms might be too narrow in scope and might also lead to a serious weakening of those services excluded from the proposed family service. Services for mentally ill, physically handicapped and elderly people were to be excluded, except where – like the home helps – they also catered for families with children. In the latter instance those services were to be taken over *en bloc*.

This concern was epitomised in a lecture given by Professor Titmuss at the Royal Society of Health Congress in April, 1965.[19] He argued instead for 'a structural re-organisation which places emphasis on social service rather than on biological or sociological criteria – like the family', which would provide services 'irrespective of age, family background and relationships' and which would 'bring together within one administrative structure all social workers in the employ of a single authority'.[20]

As a result a small group of people who were influential in the social services came together to put pressure on the government for an inquiry into the organisation of the personal social services before reforms were decided upon. The climax to this pressure was a memorandum to Mr Douglas Houghton urging a speedy review by an independent committee. The signatories included: Miss G. Aves, former Principal Welfare Officer at the Ministry of Health and a governor of the National Institute for Social Work Training, Mr R. Huws Jones, Principal of the National Institute for Social Work Training and former Vice-Chairman of the Younghusband Working Party, Professor J. Morris, Director of the Social Medicine Research Unit at the London School of Hygiene and Tropical Medicine, Mr T. Raison, Editor of *New Society*, Mr D. Jones of the National Institute for Social Work Training and Chairman of the Standing Conference of Organisations of Social Workers, Professor Richard Titmuss of the London School of Economics, Miss Margery Taylor of the London Boroughs Training Committee and Mr Lewis Waddilove, secretary of the Joseph Rowntree Memorial Trust. Mr Huws Jones and Professor Morris were, in addition, members of a small advisory group set up by the Minister of Health (Mr Kenneth Robinson), while Professor Titmuss was a member of the Royal Commission on Medical Education and was asked, shortly afterwards, to advise the Secretary of State for Scotland on the reform of local authority social work services.

The pressure succeeded. The White Paper, 'The Child, The Family and the Young Offender',[21] appeared in August 1965 with detailed proposals for replacement of juvenile and domestic courts with family courts and family councils. It also gave notice that the government intended to appoint a small, independent committee to examine the organisation of local authority social services.

One can only speculate on the reasons and events behind this governmental change of heart. Certainly Miss Bacon was known to favour speedy reform. Mr Houghton's speech to the House of Commons on the second reading of the Local Authority Social Services Bill notes his own close involvement and also indicates some of the problems of divided ministerial responsibility which had to be overcome. He commented: 'Since I was the Minister originally responsible for setting up the Seebohm Committee it was a strange experience as a co-ordinating Minister doing all the work and having all the responsibility for appointing the committee to find that constitutionally the committee had to be appointed by the Home Secretary and serviced by the Minister of Housing and Local Government'.[22]

MEMBERSHIP AND TERMS OF REFERENCE OF THE COMMITTEE

The Committee was appointed on 20 December 1965 'to review the organisation and responsibilities of the local authority personal social services in England and Wales, and to consider what changes are desirable to secure an effective family service'.

The terms of reference were thus tightly drawn. They precluded investigation of central government responsibility, despite the fact that the Home Secretary, the Secretary of State for Education and Science, the Minister of Health and the Minister of Housing and Local Government, had all to sign the declaration of appointment. They also excluded any review of the work of closely related fields outside local government, such as probation and hospital social work although local voluntary work could be examined. Finally, they were taken to mean that proposals for the removal of any services from local government were also to be excluded.

The Committee's membership was clearly designed to exclude those with a direct personal interest in any family service, such as children's officers, medical officers of health and chief welfare officers.

For the committee's chairman the government called upon Mr Frederic Seebohm – a man who epitomised the businessman-philanthropist upon which such committees have relied so much in the past. Mr Seebohm was, and is, a highly successful banker, a member of the famous Rowntree family and a trustee of the Joseph Rowntree Memorial Trust and Chairman of the National Institute for Social Work Training.

The two local authority officers, Messrs Lane and Barrett, were Clerks of a county and a county borough respectively. Mr Simson, secretary of the National Corporation for the Care of Old People, had the dual recommendation of coming from a voluntary body and having an interest in the elderly. This neatly complemented Mrs Serota's experience as a former Labour chairman of the London County Council's Children's Committee, deputy chairman of the Inner London Education Authority and a member of the Longford study group on crime. She was also, at that time, a member of the ill-fated Royal Commission on the Penal System – set up in 1964 by Henry Brooke, the then Home Secretary, and disbanded in 1966 – and was serving on the Latey Committee on the Age of Majority. Lady James had relatively little direct experience of the services concerned, although she was a juvenile court magistrate and a manager of an approved school. Her husband, Lord James of Rusholme, was President of the National Institute of Social Work Training.

The other four members were academics. Mr Huws Jones and Professor Morris had both been members of the pressure group which had campaigned for the committee's establishment and were associated with health and welfare work and social medicine respectively. Professor Morris was also a member of the Royal Commission on the Penal System. Dr Parker and Mr Leonard had both been social workers. Dr Parker was at that time a lecturer in Professor Titmuss's Department of Social Administration at the London School of Economics, but had worked closely with Professor Donnison of that department, who was one of the most persistent campaigners for a family service. Dr Parker had been a child-care officer and his doctoral thesis concerned decision-making with regard to foster-home placements.[23] Finally, Mr Leonard had trained as a psychiatric social worker and was a social work teacher at Liverpool University.

News of the committee's membership was not greeted with universal approval. The editor of *Case Conference* wrote: 'To say that many social workers are very perturbed about the make-up of the committee would be putting it mildly. We are told from various sources that the aim has been to appoint a truly independent committee and not a collection of vested interests, but there is much to be said for clearly identifiable vested interests, for at least they can be allowed for'.[24] The lack of a major doyen of social work and the influence of the National Institute were both commented upon by social workers, particularly when most of the meetings were held at the National Institute and Mr Leonard joined its staff during the committee's existence.

Overt medical reaction to the committee's appointment was almost completely non-existent. *Public Health* had earlier carried an editorial to 'The Child, The Family and the Young Offender', without mentioning the proposal for the committee to be established.[25] Neither that journal nor the *British Medical Journal* made any comment on the membership during the two months which followed its announcement. After the committee had reported the *British Medical Journal* claimed: 'The absence from the committee of at least one medical officer of health and a family doctor is remarkable in view of its terms of reference.'[26] Such comment came rather late in the day.

Certainly the presence of only one doctor was remarkable. It may be that the lack of close contact between the main body of the medical profession and the Local Authority Services Division of the Ministry of Health contributed to this omission. The membership also lacked anyone with professional experience in education outside the universities.

It is difficult to judge the effect of these omissions on the committee's work. At the very least, however, the committee was open to the charge of lack of expertise in certain fields – a change which was frequently levelled at its report. The *British Medical Journal* stated: 'Too often the report shows little knowledge of how the family doctor deals with social as well as medical problems.'[27] Lady Plowden noted that: 'There seems to be some lack of appreciation in the report of the wider meaning of education.'[28]

A. Sinfield's criticism was much more swingeing. He claimed that:

'The public and private reaction of the vested interests to the Seebohm Report cannot but heighten anxiety that a major function of the Report has been to strengthen the position of the (social work) profession and of its administrators. The committee itself consisted essentially of the various vested interests particularly from the National Institute of Social Work Training, the staff college of the social work profession'.[29]

METHODS OF WORKING

The original intention was that the committee should report very quickly. At one stage mention was made of a report within six months and the committee's own aim was to try to report within a year. It was organised around this assumption, being given no research capability and having only part-time members. On various occasions suggestions were made that members should be seconded full-time to its work for short intensive periods. These suggestions were not taken up by the Ministers concerned.

The burden of the committee's work naturally fell most heavily upon those members whose other commitments were most flexible. It was fortunate (and fortuitous) that Dr Parker was on sabbatical leave from the London School of Economics during 1966–7. He was eventually paid to work for one day a week during the committee's existence, his salary being met by the Ministry of Housing and Local Government.

In the event it took two and a half years to produce the report. Given the size of the task, this length of time was not excessive but it did greatly exceed the original expectations. At one time a two-stage report was considered, the first stage being concerned with organisational changes and thus relieving the pressure for speedy answers. This was rejected since it was felt that proposals for administrative change should be seen to grow out of those concerning changes in function. The delay clearly caused considerable embarrassment to members. In his foreword to the report the Chairman calls for serious study to be given to 'ways of meeting the burden that members carry, so as to ensure that the reports are produced as quickly as possible'.

The committee's secretary, Mr P. I. Wolf, was a Principal in the Ministry of Housing and Local Government, where he had been since 1955. The later years of his service had been spent with the Local Government Commission for England. He had no direct experience of work in the personal social service field.

The Civil Service appears to have been similarly embarrassed by the delay in the report's appearance. Mr Wolf was promoted to Assistant Secretary in the Local Government Re-organisation Division of the Welsh Office in Cardiff early in 1968. This move can hardly have helped the committee's work despite his prodigous efforts.

In the debate on the second reading of the Local Authority Social Services Bill, Mr Houghton also stated: 'I know that the arrangements for servicing this committee to begin with were not at all satisfactory.'[30] It is impossible to judge whether he was referring to the lack of paid members, the secretarial arrangements or the accommodation. The committee quickly forsook its official home at the Ministry of Housing and Local Government in favour of the National Institute for Social Work Training for all but the taking of oral evidence. This move would not have materially reduced their contact with the appropriate civil servants, since these worked in the Ministry of Health and the Home Office.

The final report was written by the members of the committee themselves, with Dr Parker acting as editor.

It is arguable that, had the committee realised how long it would take to produce the report, they would have wished to commission research. It is equally clear that a research programme could have been no part of the bargain of a speedy report in return for the committee's very existence. Members must have been aware of this constraint when accepting the invitation to serve. A small project by Bleddyn Davies was in fact commissioned, but it did not appear in the final report, nor did it form the basis for any of the committee's proposals. Reference to it will be made later.

The committee began work in January 1966 and met on seventy-four occasions. It invited views from local authorities and other interested bodies and individuals on the strength of the case for organisational change, the form of any proposed changes, their likely repercussions and the timing and method of implementation of any changes. The invitation was made in February and replies were requested by the end of April, which allowed relatively little time for careful thought and consideration. In addition, local authorities were asked to document and comment upon any changes or experiments that they had undertaken.

Committee members also visited, between them, seventeen local authorities. These authorities were selected as being broadly representative in size, type, geographical location and organisational arrangements. They also included a number which were known to be conducting interesting and experimental work. The normal procedure was for an authority to be visited by two or three committee members.

The committee began taking oral evidence at an early stage in its proceedings and continued to do so for approximately one year. Representatives from forty-two organisations and a number of individuals were seen, although in many instances only about half the committee members were present at these meetings. This was a deliberate attempt to reduce the workload of the committee. Regular meetings of the full committee took place concurrently during which written and oral evidence was considered. Occasional full-scale discussions were also held to review overall progress, to discuss major problems or to map out future lines of inquiry. These discussions usually centred around conceptual discussion papers prepared by members – frequently Dr Parker. Such meetings normally extended over two days.

Once the bulk of the oral evidence had been taken and the main possibilities for reform had been outlined the committee split into informal study groups on crucial problem issues and services. Topics such as specialisation and training, links with the education services and with housing were all dealt with in this way. Many of the informal discussions with outside experts occurred in these small groups. A similar procedure was adopted for drafting particular sections of the final report. The informality of these study groups precludes any thorough assessment of their role.

Before discussing the evidence and the committee's eventual recommendations, account should be taken of two further factors which greatly complicated its work.

First, in addition to the pressure from Ministers to produce an early report, many other developments were occurring while the committee was sitting. There were, for example, several other inquiries on closely related topics – notably the Plowden inquiry on Children and Their

Primary Schools,[31] the Maud committee on Management of Local Government[32] which reported in 1967, the Royal Commission on Local Government 1966–9,[33] the Royal Commission on Assize Courts[34] and the Summerfield Working Party on Psychologists in the Education Services.[35] Then again preparation of a new White Paper on Children in Trouble[36] was proceeding simultaneously with the committee's work as were the development of ideas for preventing family break-up later to be enshrined in the Community Development Projects. Talk of health service re-unification was also in the air – to be confirmed in 1967 and given tentative form in the first Green Paper[37] published on the same day as the Seebohm Report. Similarly, the creation in 1966 of the new Department of Social Security and with it the Supplementary Benefits system brought with it ideas for a wider visiting service by the Supplementary Benefit Commissions officers. Finally, a number of local authorities were experimenting with new patterns of internal organisation based on departmental amalgamations: in these, social workers saw the spectre of subordination to the Medical Officer of Health. This was particularly true in London where, late in the committee's deliberations, the London Boroughs' Management Services Unit proposed re-organisation under the Medical Officer of Health. The Home Secretary explained to the House of Commons that he could not prevent this, but advised authorities to delay change. 'Waiting for Seebohm' had become a major pre-occupation in the social services.

One development did, however, give the committee an advantage. Events in Scotland preceded those in England. In response to the Kilbrandon Report the Minister announced his intention to legislate both on the setting up of 'children's panels' and on re-organisation of the personal social services. He set up a working party of local authority representatives and civil servants, advised by Professor Titmuss and others, to draw up proposals for re-organisation of the local authority social work services. The results of this appeared in a White Paper[38] in October, 1966, and an Act[39] combining these two reforms was finally passed just as the Seebohm Report appeared. Although there were differences (the probation service, included in Scotland, was outside the Seebohm terms of reference), these events did at the very least provide a guide to the likely response to reform proposals. They may well have been of greater influence. Professor Titmuss was one of the first people to give evidence to the committee and, insofar as was possible, the eventual proposals for reorganisation bore a marked similarity.

The developments outlined above clearly led to a second major problem: however closely the committee's terms of reference were drawn their proposals were bound to have important implications on matters outside their immediate remit, especially as the report betrays marked reluctance to be bound by those terms of reference. Many members had close links with these related fields and were naturally concerned that the full implications were taken into account. The degree of restriction upon local authorities' freedom of action, the future of the public health departments, the place of the probation service and of pre-school play-groups were all matters upon which some members had very strong views. Yet it was felt, by the Chairman in particular, that any notes of dissent would seriously weaken the committee's impact. In extreme cases, therefore, a form of words was arrived at which noted that a range of views was held, whilst emphasising the points of agreement. Despite the eggshells underfoot the committee was thus able to present a united face. This proved to be one of the Report's most important political strengths.

Given the difficulties under which it laboured the committee could have been forgiven had it felt itself to be besieged. The committee commented (para 50) that '. . . a situation in which five bodies appointed by central government . . . are examining inter-related problems but from different standpoints and within different time scales presents difficulties both for the members of the bodies concerned, and for the organisations which have to prepare evidence for them'.

RESEARCH EVIDENCE

Since the committee was unable to sponsor any major research programme the existing research evidence became crucial. There were very major gaps in this evidence.

Studies did exist which demonstrated the inadequacies of existing organisational structure, notably those by Donnison,[40] Rodgers and Dixon[41] and Jefferys.[42] These highlighted the lack of unified policy and the difficulties in achieving such a policy among different agencies, the confusion among the general public as to who did what, wasteful duplication of functions, poor co-operation between different workers and difficulties of attracting staff to small departments. They did not however, provide any experimental evaluation of one form of organisation against another.

The possibility of some such evaluation did, however, exist in that health and welfare departments were combined in some local authorities and separate in others. Bleddyn Davies, of the London School of Economics, was at that time working on the relationship of needs to resources in local authorities. He was given a small grant by the Ministry of Housing and Local Government to enable him to speed up his work and to see if it could be adapted to examining the relative performance of combined and separately organised departments. The research was of a sophisticated statistical nature and it was of course limited to examining the inputs of services rather than their effectiveness. It was difficult to comprehend and the results proved to be inconclusive. It was not published as part of the report, nor did it form any major part of the committee's argument.[43]

The committee did consider a proposal that research and experiment should precede a final decision. It saw:

'grave and, in our judgement, over-riding objections to this approach . . . First, there is the difficulty of setting up and evaluating true experiments in this complex field; second, the time required would only prolong the uncertainty about the future which has followed the setting up of this enquiry. This is damaging morale in the services and discouraging progressive development. Third, we doubt whether such experiments in this particular field would produce clear and reliable results' (para 115).

As R. Holman[44] points out, research into social work itself is similarly inconclusive. Little is known of what actually occurs when social workers meet clients or groups of clients, or of the reasons why particular decisions on whether or how to help clients are made. The outcomes of social work have only been evaluated in crude terms and this is equally true of decisions as to what sort of help is most appropriate in any particular situation. A. Sinfield[45] claims, in fact, that the Seebohm report 'never appears to question the efficacy of social work'.

Some studies of how social workers spend their time do exist[46] but they too are unsophisticated: they paralleled studies of other occupations in showing that much time is spent in relatively unproductive work and much of the productive work does not demand high skills.

Sinfield also examines studies of the extent to which known needs remain unmet and finds that they cover only certain types of need and are frequently based on small, local investigations. The Seebohm Committee had often to resort to generalisations such as 'services for the physically handicapped are in urgent need of development' (para. 319) and 'the present services are falling far short of meeting the extent of need . . . although it is difficult to measure accurately the amount by which they fall short' (paras 173 and 174). The committee did engage Miss Jean Packman and Mr Michael Power to bring together the work done on different forms of social, emotional and physical handicap among children and the results are published as Appendix Q to the report. They estimated that one child in ten needed some form of special help whereas one child in twenty-two actually received it. They did not, however, solve the problem of overlap between various studies, so that the estimate is tentative.

Finally, consumer research hardly existed. The committee itself regretted that it was 'unable to sound consumer reaction to the services in any systematic fashion' (para. 43).

Given this lack of data, it is hardly surprising that the committee was unable to make definitive judgements on whether its own proposals would do most towards securing the 'effective family service' which its terms of reference required. Instead, it was forced to take fairly generalised objectives – such as the prevention of family breakdown and the rehabilitation of families which have broken down – to examine the *prima facie* case concerning the effectiveness and efficiency of existing services and then argue on *à priori* grounds about the relative merits of different solutions.

The committee was, however, concerned to build better evaluation and research procedures into any new organisation which it proposed. It devoted a chapter of its report to research, in which it commented: 'We cannot emphasise too strongly the part which research must play in the creation and maintenance of an effective family service. Social planning is an illusion without adequate facts; and the adequacy of services mere speculation without evaluation' (para. 473).

One can only regret that the committee, too, was caught up in a situation which demanded action before evaluation and experiment. In its own defence it stated: 'Ideally (research) should precede change; practically it becomes possible only when problems are identified and investigated sufficiently early and machinery exists for continuous research to be undertaken' (para. 116).

THE EVIDENCE RECEIVED AND THE RECOMMENDATIONS

(a) Organisational
The committee's request for evidence was directed almost exclusively at the adequacy of existing organisational structures and at proposals for change.

The majority of interest groups who submitted evidence were strongly critical of existing arrangements, citing the by then familiar stories of confusion, multi-visiting, buck-passing and poor co-ordination. They strongly favoured radical reform, as did a minority of local authorities.

There was naturally much less agreement on the form that any reform should take. The proposals centred around seven possibilities: experiment before national reform; more formal co-ordination of existing departments; two separate social service departments for children and their families and for old people and handicapped adults; a similar scheme but with the services for the elderly and handicapped being combined with the health departments; a social casework department acting as agent for other services; the personal social services to be absorbed into health or health and education departments, and finally a comprehensive social service department. The committee discusses the relative merits of these proposals in Chapters 6 and 7 of its report.

Many of these proposals had been mooted before the report, as had a further plan by Mrs Jefferys[47] for social work services to be centred around three major areas – the schools, health units based on general practice and an enlarged children's department. Had the committee set up these proposals as possible models of development, one might have seen what the evidence conspicuously lacked – a comparative evaluation of different proposals by the interest groups concerned. Instead, proposals were submitted with little evaluation of their strengths and weaknesses and comparison between proposals was limited to the oral evidence. Committee members have remarked on the changes in some groups' evidence between the written and oral stages.

The balance of the evidence from the various interested bodies was heavily weighted in favour of a unified social services department quite separate from the health department. This was particularly true of the social worker organisations and the bodies closely connected with social work. They voted almost unanimously for this proposal – some expressing strong opposition to the prospect of control by the Medical Officer of Health. Clearly there were minor variations: those closely connected with services for children, for example, were concerned lest the advances in their service be lost in wholesale reform and (somewhat naïvely) suggested a phased take-over of other activities. Nonetheless the main message was very clear.

Similar proposals were submitted by such bodies as the County Councils Association and the Society of Clerks. The former body laid particular emphasis on the effective development of social work as a distinct profession.[48]

In contrast the evidence from medical and para-medical bodies lacked this unity of purpose. The Medical Officers of Health themselves were against radical change, preferring a gradual evolution towards better staffing and combined health and welfare departments. It was notable that the trend amongst the health visitors and nurses on the staff of the health departments was towards attachment to general practice – a situation which was not applicable to all social workers. Investigation by the committee failed to produce any evidence that existing combined health and welfare departments provided a better or worse service than separate departments.

In the event the committee came down strongly in favour of a unified social service department, which would have:

'responsibilities going well beyond those of existing local authority departments, but they will include the present services provided by children's departments, the welfare services provided under the National Assistance Act 1948, educational welfare and child guidance services, the home help service, mental health social work services, other social work services provided by health departments, day nurseries and certain social welfare work currently undertaken by some housing departments' (para. 3).

Arguments that weighed heavily with the committee included: the need for a single point of responsibility for social care; the need for concentration on the development of social care; the need for a powerful department both to secure resources and to ensure co-operation with others on an equal footing. The committee also admitted that 'in the case of the medical officers of health, mutual misunderstanding with social workers has gone so far as to be a significant factor in our overall thinking on the future shape of the social services' (para. 691).

In considering the viability of such a new organisation the committee were bound to examine in some detail how the proposed department might operate. They were strongly taken with the idea of locally accessible centres for fieldwork teams which was current at the time and which many organisations recommended. Clearly, in a unified organisation this became more possible. But the proposals were more crucially affected by whether it was possible for fieldworkers of differing backgrounds to take on a wide range of currently specialist functions. This was not merely a question of a common basis for social work method. It also involved knowledge of a wide range of complex legislation, a familiarity with many local services which were closely linked with the personal social services, and the establishment of co-operative relationships with many workers in those services who had previously been used to working with a smaller number of specialist social workers. If this were not possible then one of the major arguments in favour of unification – that the family should be treated as a unit without a multiplicity of social workers being involved – was considerably weakened. The Committee considered this issue of specialisation and the attendant implications for social work training in considerable depth. The problems were most acute with those services having a social work content but close working relationships outside the proposed social services department. These included educational welfare and housing welfare, local authority mental health services, child guidance, probation and hospital social work. In the face of conflicting evidence, the committee came down in favour of inclusion within the new department wherever possible. Probation and hospital social work were outside the terms of reference and the committee had to content itself with calling for urgent review of these services in the light of its proposals. In recommending inclusion of welfare services in housing and education the committee were strongly influenced by the evidence of lack of development in these fields. The mental health services offered a more complex problem, a point of particular concern being whether the medical profession would be prepared to exchange confidential information with social workers who were not subordinate to the medical officer of health. Medical evidence was far from united on this point.

The decisions on these issues were in line with the committee's views that, since the need for co-operation between services was inevitable, inter-dependence should be built into the system from the outset and that the stronger and more comprehensive the new department, the more chance it had of achieving proper co-operation with other services.

Nonetheless doubts remain about their proposals for a mixture of general purpose social workers and specialists on long-term attachment to other agencies.

Similar problems surrounded the allocation of residential institutions. The use of residential facilities is an integral part of social care and yet the dividing line between social and health care is extremely blurred. This dividing line had already become something of an iron curtain where elderly people were concerned, and the quality of treatment had suffered in consequence. The committee suggested concurrent powers for the health and social services as one means of resolving the dilemma. In this instance duplication of services appeared to be unavoidable.

The relationship between central and local government was a matter upon which a number of politically sensitive recommendations were made.

Firstly, given its proposal for a unified local service, the committee was adamant in supporting the call for a corresponding single responsibility at central level. This was despite the fact that it had been firmly told to confine itself to local re-organisation. The logic of the situation was clearly irrefutable.

The recommendations for central influence over local authority services were equally fraught. The local authorities were highly sensitive to proposals for limitations on their freedom of action, particularly in the light of the Maud Committee report which was strongly critical of existing ministerial controls. The case for central government inspection and in the early years, for a statutory committee would have been accepted. Indeed the County Councils Association proposed a statutory committee in its own evidence. Much less acceptable was the proposal that the Minister should have a right of veto on the appointment of the head of the new department. The committee itself was divided on this issue, some members rejecting any greater compulsion than for the local authorities to consult the Minister. The majority, however, stuck out for the ministerial veto, at least for the initial appointment.

As to the background of the heads of the departments, the committee recommended that 'the objective should be to secure that most . . . are people professionally qualified in social work . . . or administrators with qualifications in social work' (para. 620). They recognised, however, the shortage of suitable applicants and suggested a degree of flexibility in applying any rules about qualification.

(b) Timing

The recommendations for the timing of proposed reforms were also matters likely to arouse opposition in local government circles and elsewhere.

Suggestions for phasing of reform had little to commend themselves politically: some authorities might drag their feet and the gradual absorbtion of small services would be bound to appear as a take-over by those fortunate enough to be in on the ground floor. The bitterness and uncertainty created would be far more disruptive than the initial confusion of wholesale re-organisation.

More powerful were the proposals that social service reform should occur at the same time as local government reform. This point was particularly stressed by the local authorities and their associations. There were strong arguments in its favour, particularly when it became clear that the health services were to be reorganised at the same time. If there were to be large-scale unitary authorities it was wasteful to establish highly-paid posts in existing authorities. If social services were to be at the lower of a two-tier structure, appointments to large existing county authorities would prove something of an embarrassment. Finally, the Medical Officers of Health would not have some years in limbo waiting to depart to the proposed Area Health Boards.

The arguments against this proposition were also strong, however, and were bound to have an appeal to a group of highly committed people who had laboured hard and long to hammer out proposals and were determined to see them implemented. The situation in the services would be highly likely to deteriorate if major and hence unsettling proposals were to hang over peoples heads for any length of time. Development of services could well be disrupted and people opposed to Seebohm's recommendations might take action to frustrate them. The report of the London Boroughs' Management Services Unit showed how far this was possible. If delay were prolonged – and this was certainly possible with any major reform of local government – the Seebohm proposals would surely lose some of their political force. Finally, local authority members and officers, pre-occupied with the complexities and inevitable inter-authority disputes over local government reform, would hardly spare the time to nurture the Seebohm department during its birth and early infancy.

Not surprisingly, therefore, the committee recommended that wholesale reform be implemented as soon as possible.

(c) Resources and review of existing services
Chapters 8 to 12 of the report comprise a review of existing services within the committee's purview. They take in services for children, old people and the remaining personal services in local health departments.

It is a measure of the preoccupation with organisational reform of existing services that the committee received virtually no evidence on the needs of young people – particularly for counselling and related services. It recognised this gap – and the opportunity such services offered for preventive work with future parents – much too late in its deliberations. The chapter on the needs of young people became, in the words of one of its members, 'the chapter we never wrote'. The committee was forced to content itself with a call for a further inquiry.

Of the services which were reviewed, the outstanding picture presented was of sheer inadequacy of the resources to tackle the problems with which they were faced. Such a view was inescapable despite the inadequacy and circumstantial nature of the evidence. Indeed, the committee argued that, since the services had not normally gone out to discover needs and since the expressed need was likely to be limited by people's low expectations of receiving service, the complexity of the welfare jungle and other factors, then any true expression of needs was likely to far exceed existing estimates.

The committee made it clear that an 'effective family service' was impossible without a major expansion of resources. Paragraph 24, however, states:

'The report is concerned throughout with resources: how the existing resources can best be used; what additional resources are likely to be available; how these additional resources can be attracted. An effective family service cannot be provided without additional resources. It would be naïve to think that any massive additional resources will be made available in the near future. . . .'

This gives the key to the committee's strategy. They painted in the picture of unmet needs but they refrained from spelling out the full implications in terms of financial and manpower costs. The full evidence was not available but that which existed was frightening and to spell it out in detail would have been politically unwelcome at a time of financial stringency and cuts in public expenditure. Its other proposals might therefore be shunned. The committee seems to have preferred instead to concentrate on achieving the first base of a unified department, from which the struggle for more resources could be better waged. Townsend,[49] in particular, has criticised this strategy, arguing that the extent of unmet needs should have been investigated and publicised. One can only speculate as to who was right.

(d) A new philosophy

In keeping with other reviews of its type – notably the Plowden Report on primary education, – the committee also gathered together many of the progressive ideas of its time and presented them into a coherent philosophy designed to guide the new department in its operation. The chapters on research, prevention and the community exemplify this approach. They breathe life into the committee's avowed intention to create:

'. . . a community-based family-oriented service, which will be available to all. This new department will . . . reach far beyond the discovery and rescue of social casualties; it will enable the greatest possible number of individuals to act reciprocally, giving and receiving service for the well-being of the whole community' (para. 2).

They were clearly designed to lead opinion in the new service they proposed.

EVENTS AFTER THE REPORT WAS PUBLISHED:

Reactions to the report were in part predictable. It was widely welcomed by the social worker organisations who urged speedy legislation. Many academics in the social administration field gave it an equally warm welcome: Professor Donnison called it 'a great State paper'.[50] The more radical academics criticised it as a social workers' rather than a consumers' charter.

Its proposals on training were the only ones to be met with major criticism by social workers. These had called for a single central advisory council on personal social services which would have a standing committee on training. Close links with the central government department would therefore have been allowed. The editor of *Case Conference*, however, led the call for 'an independent body' concerned with training for social work, claiming that 'it would be highly dangerous if the provision of services, the recruitment and selection of workers, their training and their qualifications were all centred in one depart-ment'.[51]

Medical reaction indicated mixed feelings. The British Medical Association announced that 'we cannot accept the view implied in this Report that the Medical Officer of Health is not suited to direct the proposed Social Services Department. Indeed, we consider it essential that the new Department should be under his direction'. One anonymous medical officer of health called it 'a national disaster' and the *British Medical Journal* stated that 'the transfer to lay staff of medical and social functions now carried out by doctors raises questions of principle which are of concern to all doctors'.[52]

But the doctors were distracted by the simultaneous appearance of the Green Paper on re-organisation of the National Health Service. The *Medical Officer*, for example, called speculation on the appointment of medical officers of health to head the proposed social services depart-ments 'an academic exercise in the light of the Green Paper', and it noted that 'the two documents do in fact link up well together'.[53]

Many appear to have accepted Dr J. Gilloran's advice in the choice between deciding to 'imitate King Canute against the social work tide' or to 'accept Seebohm and direct their energies towards securing a prominent place for preventive medicine in the re-organised structure of the National Health Service'.[54]

The medical profession continued to press its opposition to the report's proposals, particularly through the Public Health Committee of the British Medical Association. Yet it did so without apparent enthusiasm, without any serious alternative proposals and, one suspects, without any great hope of success. Its main concern seems to have been to delay implementation of the proposals until reform of the National Health Service took place.

Other organisations expressed broad sympathy with the report, except where it impinged directly upon their interests. The British Psychological Society for example condemned the section of the report dealing with the education services in general and the child guidance service in particular.[55] *The Justice of the Peace and Local Government Review* opposed the requirement for ministerial approval of the proposed directors of social services.[56]

There followed a period of intense lobbying, especially by social workers. A Seebohm Implementation Group was established, with Mr D. T. White as chairman, which included representatives from the social work services affected by the report. Committee members toured the country explaining their proposals.

The central government, not unnaturally, lapsed into silence. The Home Office Children's Department were heavily concerned with the business leading up to the Children and Young Persons' Act, 1969: Ministers were still considering whether reform should be delayed until local government re-organisation and some considerable embarrassment had been caused by the committee's insistence upon a unified responsibility in central government. Debates on the report occurred in both Houses of Parliament, during which speakers pressed for a Government statement of intent.

In these circumstances it was indeed fortuitous that Mrs Serota had left the committee late in its deliberations to join the House of Lords as Baroness in Waiting. On the untimely death of Mr Stephen Swingler she became Minister of State in the Department of Health and Social Security, with Mr David Ennals moving over to be responsible for social security. Her intimate knowledge of the committee's work and her links with local government and with the children's service enabled her to play a leading role in government discussions on reform. In this she was assisted by Professor Abel-Smith of the London School of Economics, who was acting as personal adviser to Mr Crossman, Secretary of State for Health and Social Security.

During the delay some local authorities – notably Ealing, Sutton and Greenwich – put forward reform plans which combined health, children's and welfare services under their medical officers of health. This only served to intensify pressure for the government to act on the report.

The pressure succeeded: ministers were persuaded that neither the situation painted in the report nor the uncertainty which it had created were tolerable. The attractions to them of significant legislation after so much frustration in other fields must also have been considerable.

A small Inter-Departmental Social Work Group of civil servants was established to draft a bill and to service its implementation.

The bill, when it appeared, was something of an anti-climax. It was a machinery bill, transferring existing powers and duties from existing local authority departments to the new one. This approach was taken because to enact new powers would have involved careful delineation of these powers in relation to the existing powers of related agencies. There was insufficient time to do this. The approach had its drawbacks, no mention could be made of educational welfare services for example, since these services were enshrined as a statutory function only insofar as school attendance work was concerned. Similarly there was no general power to promote social welfare, for which social workers had hoped and which the Scottish legislation had included. Nor was anything said about central government responsibilities – over which point confusion and speculation reigned. Finally, not until one read the accompanying Green Paper on The Future of the National Health

Service did one become aware that the division between the two was to be based on the 'primary skill' employed.

The bill had a remarkably easy passage through Parliament. The committee and the social work organisations had been equally assiduous in their wooing of the Conservative Party: Sir Frederic Seebohm, in fact, lived in the Hertford constituency of Lord Balniel, Opposition spokesman on social services. In a sparsely attended House of Commons debate on the second reading of the Bill[57] hardly a word was said to contradict the Seebohm proposals. The demarcation between health and social services was generally thought to be correct, although it was recognised that this was necessarily arbitrary and fears were expressed lest it became an iron curtain. Opposition and Labour criticisms centred around three points. The lack of a general clause to promote welfare was noted and the Opposition pledged itself to 'breathing life into the Bill' by having such a clause included. The lack of parallel central government re-organisation was roundly condemned. Mr Marcus Worsely accused the Government of being 'a bigamist preaching monogamy' and Mr Houghton among others suspected that 'the Home Secretary wants to stick to his children, otherwise he will be asscoiated with the police and crime'. Members also expressed anxiety at the extent of central government control over local government. The Bill followed the Seebohm committee by laying down a statutory committee to which only matters concerning the personal social services could be referred and by giving a Ministerial right of veto on appointments to posts of director of social services.

A consultative document on the reorganisation of training and advisory councils, which accompanied the Bill, incorporated the amendments to the Seebohm training proposals which the social work organisations had requested.

The Bill went through all its Parliamentary changes virtually unchanged. Last ditch efforts to amend it by the medical profession, as well as Opposition amendments were waived in Committee and at the third reading so that it could become law before Parliament was dissolved.

The Inter-Departmental Social Work Group produced guidelines to local authorities on the implementation of the new Act and the appointed day for its full introduction was fixed as 1 April, 1971.

Much of the initial concern was with the appointment of directors of social services. Circular 1/70 of the Inter-Departmental Social Work Group advised authorities that directors should have experience in administration of the local authority social services and should preferably be professionally qualified in social work. A small number of authorities attempted to appoint people outside this field – usually medical officers of health, members of town or county clerk's departments or people from outside local government. Some were successful, but this was usually only after a prolonged and highly-publicised battle with the responsible Minister. A study by M. J. Brown[58] and his colleagues shows that the overwhelming majority of directors had considerable experience in either local authority children's or welfare departments.

It is more difficult to generalise about the progress made in forging the new departments into a working entity, since progress has been extremely patchy. Twelve authorities had not announced the name of their new director by the appointed day and Lancashire received special dispensation to defer local implementation of the Act. Sir Frederic Seebohm has recently admitted that 'the re-organisation itself has been more painful than expected'.[59] It was to be expected that personnel and organisational changes would cause some initial deterioration in the services, although objective data is lacking on this point.

The re-organisation of central government departments, which was delayed until the Conservative Government came to power in the summer of 1970, appears to have been equally painful and disruptive. In it the old Children's Department of the Home Office was taken into the Department of Health and Social Security. As a result, strong central guidance on re-organisation was lacking and the new directors had to rely most heavily on the Seebohm Report itself.

Evidence from M. J. Brown and his colleagues, so far unpublished, suggests that most authorities have organised their fieldwork services into area teams, as the report suggested. It also shows that the Seebohm call for a proper research activity in local authority social services is eliciting a fairly positive response. The urgent need for re-training has also received some recognition. The Local Government Training Board has, for example, sponsored short emergency courses for senior personnel in the departments, in which members of the Seebohm committee have played an important part.

A large number of very major problems remain, however, and different authorities have been attempting to tackle them in different ways, with varied success. The future of social work in schools and housing departments, and the place of child guidance clinics remains uncertain. The probation service has suffered a loss of staff and its independence is threatened. But it is with the health services that the most critical issues of co-operation exist. There has been a major crisis over the use of records from the old health departments which contain confidential medical information. The organisational base for hospital social work remains at issue, with many of these workers wishing to be employed by the social services departments. Finally, the effect of the proposed re-organisation of the National Health Service, on co-operation with a re-organised local government system in the planning and provision of services is, as yet, unknown.

These difficulties in forging new relationships have been exacerbated, at least temporarily, by fieldworkers taking on a more all-purpose role. In consequence old conventions between, for example, the hospital psychiatrist and the local authority mental welfare officer have been challenged, while the unfamiliar social worker who made this challenge may have been less knowledgeable about local resources or even the law than the mental welfare officer who did the work in the past. By no means all social workers in local authority service have found the prospect of doing multi-purpose social work congenial: many departments have retained a degree of past specialisation, at least for the short term.

Social services personnel, attempting to tackle these problems and shortly to be faced in many areas with major changes which local government reform makes imminent, could be forgiven for wondering whether it was all worth while.

CONCLUSION

A fundamental review of the personal social service field was overdue by the early 1960s. There is little doubt that it would have occurred at some stage, whichever party was in power and whatever the precipitating factor turned out to be. As it was, the review was brought about by a new Labour Government impatient for widespread and rapid reform of many aspects of the Welfare State and related services. The plethora of inquiries drew an apt comment from Mr Maurice Macmillan during the second reading of the Local Authority Social Services Bill. He was reminded of the Walrus and the Carpenter:

'If seven maids with seven mops
Swept it for half a year,
Do you suppose', the Walrus said,
'That they could get it clear?'
'I doubt it' said the Carpenter,
And shed a bitter tear.[60]

The committee began as one of the lesser of these inquiries, but it produced a report which is of major potential significance. The report's chief political power was in its unity of purpose. Jarvis notes that 'committees of inquiry cannot be impartial although many of them pretend to be. The Seebohm Committee . . . makes no such pretence. Its report is a coherent, persuasive presentation of a case from one point of view'.[61]

Certainly, the logic of its proposals is attractive, but one has some sympathy with Dr Kershaw when he complains: 'The more one studies the report, the more it is evident that it consists largely of the giving of opinions on opinions and that it states only one side of a case which needs prolonged and multi-lateral discussion.'[62] The political realities of the time – not the least of which was the mutual distrust between many doctors and social workers – prevented this discussion from taking place.

One might add that the committee was careful not to prejudice acceptance of its report by including proposals, particularly about manpower and monetary resources, which the government of the day would have found embarrassing. The wisdom of this strategy can only be guessed at. As it is, the committee's arguments in favour of a more powerful department, which could command a greater share of local authority resources in return for undivided responsibility for social care, have been accepted. The latest public expenditure announcements give some slight cause for hope that they will prove to be correct. The crucial test will be whether the services to the community are improved.

There is little doubt that if the full message of the report is accepted by all, then a major improvement in services will in fact occur. Measurement of this improvement will, however, not be easy. Normal developments in services, such as the Chronically Sick and Disabled Persons Act, 1970 complicate any assessment. Furthermore, social services departments seek to meet several different objectives towards different community groups: they have, for example, both a social support and a social control function. These objectives may conflict. The first part of one study, designed to assess changes in the services to particular client groups as a result of social services re-organisation has already been carried out.[63]

What can be firmly stated, however, is that unless the new departments are able to develop proper co-operation with other services, they will fail in their work. An editorial response in *The Lancet* to Professor Titmuss's original Royal Society of Health lecture, stated: 'The modern concept of community care must be broadly based. Too many people have not yet recognised the difficulties of applying this concept to a departmental structure which has more to do with the thirties than the seventies.'[64] One might add that no re-allocation of functions between departments or organisations will solve the fundamental problems in a situation where the work of many specialists overlap. The real problems are to discover proper methods of working together between people with different professional outlooks and between departments and organisations whose interests may coincide at one point and conflict at another. Local government itself is becoming increasingly aware of these problems.[65]

The Seebohm Report resulted in strengthening the links within the personal social services. In doing so and in pressing the claims of social work as an identifiable specialism with its own separate contribution to make, the committee weakened some of the links with other specialisms. The committee made valiant attempts to build co-operative working arrangements. Some of these have been confounded, at least in the short term, by its very success in creating the strong departments which, so it argued, were needed to achieve proper co-operation. Final judgement on this and other matters must await a longer time perspective than the present allows.

NOTES

1 Committee on Local Authority and Allied Personal Social Services Report, Cmnd. 3703, HMSO, July 1968, paras, 2 and 3.
2 H. L. Wilensky, 'The Professionalisation of Everyone', *American Journal of Sociology*, September 1964.
3 The general development of these services is documented in Julia Parker, *Local Authority Health and Welfare Services*, Allen & Unwin, 1965.
4 R. M. Titmuss, *Commitment to Welfare*, Allen & Unwin, 1968, p. 85.
5 For example:
   (*a*) Report of the (Cope) Committee on Medical Auxiliaries, Cmnd. 8188, 1951.
   (*b*) Ministry of Education, Report of the (Underwood) Committee on Maladjusted Children, 1955.
   (*c*) Report of the (Ingleby) Committee on Children and Young Persons, Cmnd. 1191, 1960.
   (*d*) Report of the Royal Commission on the Law Relating to Mental Illness and Mental Defficiency, Cmnd. 169, 1957.
   (*e*) Report of the (Morison) Committee on the Probation Service, Cmnd. 1650, 1962.
   (*f*) Ministry of Health Report of the (Younghusband) Working Party on Social Workers in Local Authority Health and Welfare Services, HMSO, 1959.
6 Royal Commission on Medical Education, HMSO, 1968, paras 254 and 257.
7 Home Office Circular 157/50.
8 Report of the Care of Children Committee, 1946, Cmnd. 6922.
9 Ministry of Health: Report of the Working Party on Social Workers in the Local Authority Health and Welfare Services, 1959, (The Younghusband Report), Table 30.
10 Julia Parker and Rosalind Allen, 'Social Workers in Local Government', *Social and Economic Administration*, January, 1969, Vol. 3, No. 1, p. 17.
11 Report of the Committee on Children and Young Persons, 1960, Cmnd. 1191.
12 Ibid. para. 47.
13 D. V. Donnison and Mary Stewart, *The Child and the Social Services*, Fabian Society, 1958.

14 The Council for Children's Welfare and the Fisher Group: 'Families with Problems: A New Approach', Council for Children's Welfare, 1958.
15 D. V. Donnison, Peggy Jay and Mary Stewart: *The Ingleby Report: Three Critical Essays*, Fabian Society, 1962.
16 Report of the Scottish Advisory Council on Child Care: *Prevention of Neglect of Children*, Scottish Education Department, 1963, Cmnd. 1966.
17 Scottish Education Department, Scottish Home and Health Department: *Children and Young Persons Scotland (1964)* Cmnd. 2306.
18 *Crime – A Challenge To Us All*, Report of a Labour Party Study Group, 1964.
19 R. M. Titmuss, 'Social Work and Social Service: a Challenge for Local Government', *Royal Society of Health Journal*, April, 1965, (reproduced in *Commitment to Welfare*, op. cit., pp. 85–90).
20 Ibid., p. 90.
21 *The Child, The Family and the Young Offender*, Cmnd. 2742, HMSO, 1965.
22 House of Commons Official Report, Parliamentary Debates (Hansard), Vol. 796, No. 68, Col. 1485, 26/2/70.
23 Later published as *Decision in Child Care*, Allen & Unwin, 1966.
24 *Case Conference*, Vol. 12, No. 8, February, 1966, p. 214.
25 'Out of Court', *Public Health*, Vol. 80, No. 1, November, 1965, p. 1–4.
26 *British Medical Journal*, 3 August, 1968, p. 265.
27 Ibid. p. 266.
28 Lady Plowden, 'Schools and the Social Services Department', *Social Work*, Vol. 25, No. 4, October, 1968, p. 34.
29 A. Sinfield, 'Which Way for Social Work?' in *The Fifth Social Services*, Fabian Society, 1970, p. 41.
30 Hansard, op. cit. Col. 1486.
31 *Children and their Primary Schools*, A report of the Central Advisory Council for Education (England), HMSO, 1967.
32 Report of the Committee on the Management of Local Government, HMSO, 1967.
33 Royal Commission on Local Government in England, 1966–69, Cmnd. 4040.
34 Royal Commission on Assizes and Quarter Sessions, Cmnd. 4153, HMSO, 1969.
35 Department of Education and Science: Report of a Working Party on Psychologists in the Education Service, HMSO, 1968.
36 Home Office, *Children in Trouble*, Cmnd. 3601, HMSO, 1968.
37 Ministry of Health: *The Administrative Structure of the Medical and Related Services in England and Wales*, HMSO, 1968.
38 *Social Work and the Community*, Cmnd. 3065, HMSO, Edinburgh, 1966.
39 Social Work (Scotland) Act, 1968.
40 D. V. Donnison, *The Neglected Child and the Social Services*, Manchester University Press, 1954.
41 Barbara Rodgers and Julia Dixon, *Portrait of Social Work*, Oxford University Press, 1960.
42 Margot Jefferys, *Anatomy of Social Welfare Services*, Michael Joseph, 1965.
43 B. Davies, Research Evidence of the Committee on Local Authority and Allied Personal Social Services. It can be consulted in the Department of Environment Library. A derivative of the work has been published as *Variations in Services for Children*, Bell, 1971.
44 R. Holman, 'Social Work Research Today' in *Research and Social Work*, British Association of Social Workers Monograph No. 4, 1970.

45 A. Sinfield, 'Which Way for Social Work', op. cit. p. 28.
46 For example, Scottish Education Department, 'The Child Care Service at Work', HMSO, 1963.
   Zofia Butrym, *Medical Social Work in Action*, Bell, 1968.
47 Margot Jefferys, op. cit.
48 County Council's Association: Minutes of the Executive Council *County Council's Gazette*, Vol. 59, No. 8, August 1966, pp. 166–172.
49 P. Townsend, 'The Objectives of the New Local Service' in *The Fifth Social Service*, Fabian Society, 1970.
50 D. V. Donnison, 'Seebohm: the Report and its Implications', *Social Work* Vol. 25, No. 4, October 1968, p. 3.
51 *Case Conference*, Vol. 15, No. 4, August 1968, p. 130.
52 *British Medical Journal*, July–September 1968, p. 197.
53 *Medical Officer*, 2 August 1968, p. 69.
54 J. Gilloran: letter to *Medical Officer*, 25 October, 1968, p. 238.
55 British Psychological Society: Memorandum on the Seebohm Report and the Summerfield Report, November 1968.
56 *Justice of the Peace and Local Government Review*, August 24 and 31, 1968.
57 House of Commons Parliamentary Debates (Hansard), Vol. 796, No. 68, 26/2/1970, Cols 1406–1520.
58 M. Brown, N. Thomas and R. Thayer, 'Meet the Directors', *Municipal and Public Services Journal*, Vol. 79, No. 27. 2 July, 1971, pp. 926–929.
59 The *Spectator*, 5 February, 1972, page 217.
60 Hansard, op. cit. Col. 1500.
61 F. Jarvis, 'A View from the Probation Service', *Social Work*, Vol. 25, No. 4, October, 1968, p. 16.
62 J. D. Kershaw, *British Medical Journal*, 24 August, 1968.
63 M. J. Brown, N. Thomas and R. Thayer, Survey of Personal Social Services in the West Midlands, in process.
64 The *Lancet*, 8 May, 1965.
65 For example, J. D. Stewart, *Management in Local Government: A Viewpoint*, Charles Knight, 1971.

7 Commissions in Policy-Making

RICHARD A. CHAPMAN

The main difference between Royal Commissions and various departmental bodies, such as Commissions, Committees, and Working Parties, is in matters of prestige and status. Only about twenty-five Royal Commissions have reported since 1945 and they cover such an unclassifiable assortment of topics that it is difficult to detect any rationale at all between them and departmental bodies. It has commonly been thought that Royal Commissions have tended to be appointed to consider matters of major national importance in circumstances where a degree of independence outside the field of party political controversy is required, while in matters of lesser national significance a departmental committee is established. But a review of recent Royal Commissions throws doubt on that popular view – otherwise it is not easy to account for the following, for example, being Royal Commissions instead of departmental committees: 'Awards to Inventors'; 'Land and Population in East Africa'; 'Dundee (University College) and relationship with St Andrews University'.

There are two other general beliefs that appear to be founded on no more than rather vague assessments of precedent. Civil servants are not expected to sit on Royal Commissions, though they frequently sit on other commissions – there is no convincing reason why there should be this difference but it is clearly an advantage, on occasions, to utilise official knowledge and expertise in commission membership. There is also some general misunderstanding about powers and publicity. Departmental committees generally have no less power than Royal Commissions, for although power to send for 'persons and papers' is usually given to Royal Commissions in the royal warrant, there is no means of enforcing the power if the persons do not choose to attend and the papers are not forthcoming.[1] There is also no general rule to prevent either form of commission sitting in public or private, or deciding whether, and if so how and when, to publish some or all of the evidence presented to it.

Let there be no doubt that there is widespread confusion about these various terms. Newspapers frequently make mistakes, but so do even academic specialists in government when referring to bodies other than the one(s) they are primarily interested in at any one time. One often hears the Fulton Committee referred to as the Royal Commission on the Civil Service, the Crowther Commission as the Royal Commission on the Constitution, and the Roskill Commission as the Royal Commission on the Third London Airport.

Royal Commissions may in some respects have higher status than departmental bodies because on appointment a royal warrant is issued by the Queen and countersigned by one of the principal secretaries of state; it contains the Commission's terms of reference and its authority to call for witnesses and information. In contrast, departmental committees are appointed by the Minister concerned with the subject of the inquiry, who issues a simple letter of appointment. Where the added prestige and status of a Royal Commission evokes greater co-operation, then it may, indeed, have greater practical authority although it has no greater effective power.

It seems almost unbelievable that the various terms exist for these committees when there is so little difference between them. But careful investigation, including consultation with Machinery of Government officials in the Civil Service Department, has revealed no essential differences in the powers, structure and procedure of bodies with these different names. One might, perhaps, advance the hypothesis that the preference for departmental bodies compared with fewer Royal Commissions in recent years could be related to the increasingly important role and technical specialisation within the government bureaucracy, and that departmental bodies are more obviously creatures of departments – but research to test the hypothesis would depend on co-operation from the Civil Service, and such co-operation is at present unlikely to be available to an outsider because of the potentially sensitive issues involved. Clearly, it is a subject for urgent research within the CSD.

In a twentieth century representative democracy there is much to be said for ensuring that all aspects of government are as easily understandable as possible, and serious consideration might be given to rationalising this terminology. Thus, it might be helpful to reserve Royal Commissions for dealing with matters of constitutional significance (i.e. matters affecting the structure and functions of the organs of central and local government), and to use the term 'commission' for all other advisory or inquiring bodies intended to contribute to the policy making process. They would then still be types of committee within K. C. Wheare's[2] scheme and definition, different from other types of committee, but they would have in common their role as potentially contributing to the policy making process.

TERMS OF REFERENCE AND MEMBERSHIP

The terms of reference of a commission are set out in the royal warrant or official letter appointing it and usually take the form of a request to investigate a problem and 'make recommendations'. In all cases the appointment of members is the responsibility of the government so that in major commissions the Prime Minister and several members of the Cabinet may be involved in the selection, and in departmental committees the Minister and his advisers may make the choice. The chairman is always appointed as such, and not elected by the members from among themselves.

Normally, by the time formal letters and warrants are issued, informal agreement to serve has already been given by the members in response to no more than vague details of a general theme. At that early stage for at least two reasons there is hardly likely to be much detailed discussion of the terms of reference. First, there is the supply of willing candidates for membership. As H. McD. Clokie and J. William Robinson have explained:

> 'Fortunately, membership on a Royal Commission has been regarded as an honourable and desirable testimonial of distinction in politics, business, or scholarship. In addition to those whose public spirit involves occupying themselves in such matters, many persons are eager to serve because their interests are at stake in any economic or social change. The publicity, recognition, and influence which are accorded Royal Commissions undoubtedly keep up the supply of those willing and anxious to undertake these advisory duties'.[3]

Secondly, at the time of appointment, however well in touch they may be with the problem area, the members are unlikely to be in a position to argue about individual words and phrases in their terms of reference until they have held at least a preliminary discussion as a committee. It is usually at the first formal meeting that the commission discusses such matters as its terms of reference, how it will pursue its task, what public announcements it wishes to make, and its programme of meetings.

Perhaps it should be noted that by the time the members have an opportunity to discuss together their terms of reference events may have moved forward to a considerable extent. The ministers will have discussed the matter with their civil servants and possibly also other advisers, so that a number of people in the public administration system will have already contributed to the formulation of the task. The secretariat will have been appointed – usually a secretary and deputy secretary with clerical and typing assistance drawn from within the department concerned with the subject – and will have been involved with a certain amount of preliminary work before the commission actually meets. Indeed, with at least the Plowden Committee, some research was under way even before the members had met. In such circumstances it is hardly surprising that commissions sometimes draw attention in their final reports to the constraints imposed by their terms of reference. This was certainly the case with the Fulton Committee which commented: 'Our terms of reference excluded the machinery of government. We found at many points in our inquiry that this imposed limits on our work; questions about the number and size of departments, and their relationships with each other and the Cabinet Office, bear closely upon the work and organisation of the Civil Service'.[4]

It should not be imagined that the words in terms of reference are fixed without considerable thought, nor are they notably narrow. Thus the Fulton Committee could not consider the machinery of government because it was appointed 'to examine the structure, recruitment and management, including training, of the Home Civil Service and make recommendations' – but as it had four civil servants among its members, it would have been inappropriate to extend its terms of reference to enable it to consider such political issues as the number and size of departments and their relationship to the Cabinet. Similarly, the Redcliffe-Maud Royal Commission was appointed 'to consider the structure of Local Government in England . . . in relation to its existing functions', which prevented it from considering a reallocation of public services between local authorities and other institutions. Those who conceive and draft the terms of reference of commissions have a very important responsibility, for they are sometimes, at least in part, responsible for the success or usefulness of the whole exercise, and once fixed the system builds in a degree of rigidity that can make amendment exceedingly difficult, if not impossible.

There might be advantages in having more opportunities for commissions to secure amendments to their terms of reference as the problems they are considering become clearer; there is also always some scope for a commission to interpret its terms of reference to enable it to consider matters it feels it ought, whether or not those matters are clearly within its legal framework of reference. But either of these possibilities could make life very difficult for the government which usually wants the work done as quickly as possible, and frequent adjustment of terms of reference of commissions could be unbearably embarrassing in Parliament.

Furthermore, the members are selected with care and with a view to their expected willingness to serve, and once appointed they may feel morally obliged to work within their given terms of reference. They also tend to have in common a desire to do a useful job. Without such an element of disinterested public service (said to be noticeable even among members with obvious interests at stake) perhaps there might never be any commissions, or they would be quite different from the sort of British institutions they are. With it, in times when the work is difficult, the members may feel themselves borne over rough ground by their need to produce a report that the department or government could hope to implement.

The considerations borne in mind when selecting members to serve on commissions are complex and in some respects peculiar to the subject of particular inquiries. It is very much an exercise in compromise seen from various viewpoints. On many commissions there have to be Members of Parliament, and representatives from employers, from trade union interests, and from the academic world. Whilst it is hoped that members are not too senile, young men (however defined) are rarely thought to have established themselves sufficiently in their field, and it would generally be difficult for them to serve as membership tends to be a considerable sacrifice in terms of leisure and earnings (because they are unpaid and expenses are usually given at such a meagre rate, members are likely to be out of pocket to at least a marginal extent). Party political affiliations may be important where a government is keen to institute a particular programme of reforms – but one wonders whether it was right to appoint to the Fulton Committee the chairman of a Fabian study group without mentioning his affiliation. Previously declared positions or expertise may also need representation – but one wonders to what extent the Redcliffe-Maud Royal Commission found it helpful to have as a member someone well known to possess clearly thought out but rather inflexible attitudes to local government reform; an outsider may have doubts about the role of such a person on the Commission, about his effect on the other members and their effect on him, and subsequently question the advisability of such an appointment. Similarly with the Seebohm Committee; it may be important for a commission to make sure it has the views of those who will have to implement proposed policies – but this does not necessarily mean that so many representatives of interests should have been on the Committee. Particular interests may need to be represented – but one wonders, for example, to what extent an ex-General Secretary of the TUC could make a fresh and useful appraisal of the problems being considered by the Donovan Royal Commission (though he was probably invited especially to create a balance against other interests well represented on the Commission).

Perhaps the essence of the terms of reference and membership issues is to be found in the size of a commission and its real or apparent objectives. And, as the Departmental Committee on the Procedure of Royal Commissions observed in their report in 1910:

'A Commission selected on the principle of representing various interests starts with a serious handicap against the probability of harmony in its work, and perhaps even of practical result from its labours . . . there has been a recent tendency to make the membership of Commissions too large. The object in view is probably to ensure that various shades of opinion should be represented within the Commission, a consideration to which we attach little weight. . . . It affords little help towards administrative progress if the evidence brought before it is utilised merely to confirm prepossessions, to bolster up opinions, and to support interests'.[5]

Perhaps it is necessary in terms of fairness and the spirit of democracy to recognise more widely that people all have interests and to make their interests more explicit. Whilst it may be futile to select people for the sake of their interests and then in a somewhat arithmetical way to try to balance those interests, it may be necessary to ensure that representatives of interests whose subsequent co-operation is necessary for implementing policies are included on a commission, otherwise the inquiry may not have their confidence and the rejection of its recommendations becomes a foregone conclusion.

Whereas a committee to inquire may be looking for an answer to a particular problem, the members of a committee to advise may be selected either because they know the answers or know where to find the answers. Thus, ideally, a committee to inquire should be small; but in British government there is usually a desire for consensus, for a built-in opportunity for 'fair play', for collegiality in decision-making, so that when carried to extreme we have the example of the Plowden Committee, 'to consider primary education in all its aspects and the transition to secondary education', with as many as twenty-five members. The Fulton Committee obviously modelled aspects of its approach on its Northcote-Trevelyan predecessor, but between the two committees there were significant differences in objectives and methods of work as well as in size of membership.

Terms of reference and membership are also greatly influenced by the objectives in the minds of those responsible for setting up the commission, which may be different from the objectives understood by the members appointed to actually do the work. The Donovan Royal Commission and the Fulton Committee thus seem to have been political exercises in a more overtly party political sense than the other three commissions previously considered; but when the Seebohm Committee is seen to be working at the same time as such bodies with interrelated terms of reference as the Plowden Committee, the Redcliffe-Maud Royal Commission, and the Summerfield Working Party, one may well have serious doubts about its intended purpose.

The Plowden Committee with its very large membership is in some respects in a class of its own, at least as far as the present study is concerned. The Committee may have been too large, but it operated through working parties and study groups and its objectives seem to have been to distil the best experience and to use it to make recommendations for future improvements in primary education. Its programme of sponsored research was large, though one may wonder whether this may have been partly related to the fact that the Department of Education and Science did not really like the Committee, and the members felt they were not receiving the moral support and interest from the officials which they felt they deserved. But whether it determined its objectives and methods of working in the light of its terms of reference or because it had no choice as a result of its size and other factors, is almost a chicken and egg situation.

METHOD OF WORKING

Whilst there are no formal rules to guide the procedures of commissions there are some features common to them all, so that a pattern emerges. For example, the work may be seen in two stages: gathering information, and reporting. The informing stage always includes receiving evidence, though it should be noted that whilst submissions to commissions are described as 'evidence' and people submitting them as 'witnesses', the ordinary rules of evidence in judicial procedure do not apply and the evidence comprises opinions as well as factual information. Such hearings might be regarded as characteristic in the British system of government because they enable experts who are not members of a commission to contribute to what might be a significant stage in public policy making. The commission is enabled to hear the views of interests operating in the particular field of inquiry, and individual citizens may submit their own views. The commission will, in addition, have other methods of gathering information, but the conventional and routine method is likely to be its most time consuming – it will be recalled that the Redcliffe-Maud Royal Commission received such submissions from 2,156 witnesses.

Faced with such a large task the commission has either to lay down fairly strict guidelines on the admissibility of evidence or it may virtually delegate the task to its secretariat: which provides a further opportunity where the secretariat may have a very significant role in the whole exercise. Sometimes appointed before the individual commission members and usually from the department concerned with the subject matter of the inquiry, the secretariat may have advantages over the members in both time and experience, and although officially the servants of the commission it may, through formal and informal advice to witnesses as well as to the members individually and collectively, influence the direction and scope of the inquiry.

A third common feature in procedure is the role of the department(s) of central government. Sometimes they are involved in the service function of providing the commission with basic factual material, as did the Treasury with its Introductory Factual Memorandum for the Fulton Committee. Sometimes they help the commission by providing information at its request to enable it to reach conclusions on specific issues, as did the Department of Education and Science for the Plowden Committee. Sometimes they will present a case for consideration from the standpoint of their particular interest, as did various departments for the Redcliffe-Maud Royal Commission when they made recommendations for reducing the number of local authorities. Sometimes they present kite-flying suggestions to test the reactions from other bodies to suggested reforms, thereby forcing outside interests to formulate views on questions they had not previously considered – this was done for the Fulton Committee by the Treasury when details for reforming the Civil Service class structure were presented and evoked the views of various staff associations. Some or all of these roles may be played by departments and their representatives. Consequently there may be occasions when it may be valuable for commission members to appreciate the roles being played by departments, otherwise the commission could easily become a mere departmental creature masquerading as an independent body.

The procedure of working should be closely related to the commission's own views of its objectives, but sometimes there is doubt about the clarity of the objectives in the minds of individual members. And even when the members all have clear conceptions of their tasks, pressures of time may force them to make sacrifices to their own work programmes or resort to recommending that departments do some of the necessary research after the commission's report has been accepted.

To an outsider, especially an academic, the research programmes may sometimes appear less than completely satisfactory, but there may be several reasons for this. First, commissions tend to work under pressure of time which discourages extensive research. Secondly, there is the attitude still to be found in official circles in Britain that the social sciences in universities can contribute little of value to solving practical problems in the broad areas of general policy making (although some government departments employ social scientists to conduct specific research projects for them). Thirdly, there is little real encouragement and few precedents for commissions to appoint full-time research directors, so it is possible for members of commissions to remain fairly ignorant about what useful research *could* be done; and as a significant amount of the research that *is* done (e.g. for the commissions discussed earlier in this book) seems linked in some way with Oxford University one may wonder how much influence is being exercised by relatively few people. Fourthly, such agencies as the Government Social Survey, which is often a research agency for the commissions, has constraints on the sort of work it can do because it is staffed by civil servants; for example, for the Redcliffe-Maud Royal Commission it could not do research related to the significance of party politics in local government. Similarly the Fulton Committee could not allow it to be thought that the Committee was concerned in any way with civil servants' attitudes to party politics, and research that did incidentally touch on party politics had several passages edited out of the research report before publication.

The most important criticisms about the sponsored research follow on from combinations of these factors. The Fulton Committee seemed to accept uncritically the allegations of amateurism in the Civil Service without troubling to analyse the term 'amateur' and its significance in the context of the Service; and the Redcliffe-Maud Royal Commission seemed happy to accept statements of apparently conventional wisdom and do its work without rigorously questioning their validity and whilst ignoring party politics in local government. It may be important for an inquiry to discover and draw attention to what people think, but it is usually at least as important to discover factual information, compare the facts and the images and ensure that all relevant factors are considered in the light of the objectives of the exercise.

It is extremely difficult to assess the full cost of research for commissions, and quite misleading to assume that the costs stated in the reports (which includes payments to members and also witnesses for fares and expenses, the salary of the secretariat, the cost of any special investigations, overseas visits, and the cost of printing and publishing the report and evidence) are final or total costs. Again, there are several reasons for this. The Government Social Survey does not charge the individual commissions for whom it works, instead the costs are met as part of the running expenses of the Social Survey. There is no accepted scale for research fees so some of the sponsored research may attract a market rate (perhaps the rate applying in the costly world of business management) whilst other work, equally classified as research, is done by civil servants who are relieved of normal departmental duties to enable them to work temporarily on a specific project – so a commission may appear to get good value for money by formally sponsoring little research but having considerable uncosted work done at the expense of departments. Finally, some commissions decide not to sponsor a comprehensive research programme, but to produce a general set of guidelines, and on those occasions the main expense arises after publication of the report, when it is being decided how to give effect to the guidelines. (This was the case with the Fulton Committee, for expenses thus incurred by the Civil Service Department since the report was published could have been carried out at the expense of the Committee if it had decided to approach its task differently).

Some commissions make brief trips abroad at public expense in order to acquaint themselves with comparative experience. For example, members of the Plowden Committee visited Russia, Poland, Denmark, Sweden, France and the U.S.A., and members of the Donovan Royal Commission went to Sweden and Western Germany. But the visits in each case were so short that their value is highly questionable: more detailed and thorough comparative research might have been more valuable and less expensive – for example, one may consider the high quality of the IPCS evidence to the Fulton Committee which contained comparative studies of various countries and was subsequently published in book form.[6]

The real centre of research problems may therefore originate from the doubtful clarity of a commission's objectives. A commission to inquire should be concerned primarily with its own assessment of the problems it is considering as well as the assessments of other people however expert they may be; and in those cases when time is not of the essence it is inconceivable that this should not lead to a properly planned research programme. Secondly, when it is decided that original research would help, questions may be asked about the best way to get in touch with specialists in various fields, and how to learn about work of relevance that has already been done in Britain and overseas. Perhaps this is a function that could be fulfilled by the Social Science Research Council so that its subject panels could be made responsible for giving independent advice rather than the advice being sought from a few people with contacts in one particular university. The informal network may produce adequate results on occasions, but when research so arranged can be criticised as biased it may cast doubtful reflections on the whole of the commission's work.

The final stage in a commission's procedure concerns the method of writing the final report. This varies from commission to commission. Frequently, successive drafts are presented by the secretariat for amendment by the commission. Sometimes individual commission members (especially the chairman) write parts or the whole of the report. But in most cases the report suffers the defects of being a compromise document with consequent loss of clarity and blemishes of language, and this may become more apparent with a large commission than with a small one.

COMMISSIONS IN POLICY-MAKING

If governments expect commissions to formulate policy, commissions may constitute a negation of governmental responsibility, for it could be argued that governments should have clear ideas about what their policies should be without depending on advisory bodies for fresh ideas. Commissions may also play a significant political role if used as a method for postponing to an indefinite future decisions on questions which appear to be embarrassing but not urgent (e.g. the Crowther Commission on the Constitution); they may also have a similar political role if a government refers to them matters which are politically very controversial but lacking in consensus (e.g. the Donovan Royal Commission). Sometimes a government does not have sufficient information to formulate more than vague policy generalisations until a commission has appreciated the situation by exposing what it regards as the relevant facts,[7] and made recommendations which, even though not necessarily fully accepted, may enable the government to develop its own ideas with a greater degree of rationality and coherence (e.g. the Roskill Commission on the Third London Airport). On other occasions it requires a commission to stimulate suggestions for actions which in turn produce reactions from the many interests that may be involved in the policy area (e.g. the Fulton Committee). Almost all commissions also have an important educational role in bringing to the attention of the public some of the issues involved in a particular policy area and also in giving official sanction to the publication of officially known facts (e.g. the Fulton Committee). These and other possibilities may each on occasion explain the activities of particular commissions, but this symposium indicates that commissions can be so variegated that the value of broad generalisations becomes very doubtful.

Part of the difficulty in formulating generalisations stems from the long history of commissions which in this country can be traced back to the eleventh century (the Domesday Book may be regarded as the result of the first Royal Commission).[8] Part also stems from the way representative democracy has developed in Britain and has acquired accepted practical applications within public institutions – though the institutions have rarely been planned with that end in view. There are consequently accepted ways of doing things which, however vaguely, may be seen to embody such ideas as justice, fairness and equality, and to ensure that the will of the majority prevails and that minority rights are respected. There is also a desire to achieve the maximum degree of participation in decision-making situations.

Consider, for example, the possible democratic significance of commissions. The passage of time and the increased scope and complexities of modern government render somewhat anachronistic the Clokie and Robinson interpretation of Royal Commissions as 'a notable example of the wise combination of fact-finding and policy-forming in the modern state'.[9] The pace of governmental decision-making has advanced greatly since the inter-war period when those writers were commenting; but this does not mean that commissions may no longer have a role as representative institutions or as agents for stimulating contributions to decision-making from various interested bodies. Though we may wish to question the meaning of his word 'proper', Arthur Salter may have had a clearer appreciation of this potentially democratic role of commissions when he wrote that: 'The proper use of Advisory Bodies is the right answer of representative democracy to the challenge of the Corporative State . . . Democracy is . . . not ousted but supplemented by the advisory bodies.'[10]

In fact it seems that there is a great deal of the representative element to be found in the work of commissions. As has already been seen, the members are often selected on a basis or representativeness (however curious and biased outsiders may feel the selection of particular individuals). They are drawn from various backgrounds partly to ensure that the interests of various groups are not overlooked, but partly also to bring to bear on particular issues minds that have been trained in different professions and walks of life so that problems are analysed from a number of different viewpoints.

The opportunity for interests to present their views is also an example of the democratic element in government. Many interests take part in preparing evidence which may eventually affect policy, and if it does then the individuals or groups may feel disproportionately encouraged – people generally like to think they are doing something useful in terms of the public good.

There are various possible consequences of these theoretical approaches in terms of executive government. For example, when a government appears to reject a commission recommendation all the work may not have been in vain because the evidence may assist the government to clarify its ideas even if this is achieved through the formulation of a knock-down argument with which to disagree. Disappointing though it may be to the commissioners, does this necessarily mean that their efforts have been entirely in vain? Should they not accept stoically that that is the way government tends to work and that the nature of their exercise may be to aid the government in various possible ways to formulate its disagreement? It should never be forgotten that the government has to take into account political factors normally beyond the scope of commission terms of reference and that it is in the light of its assessment of the political environment that the government has to reach judgements about its own policies. Commissions have to work within their own institutional limitations; they are subordinate to governments.

Even if advice is given publicly through commission reports there is usually, in addition, some form of extra-governmental advice on radically new policies. Ministers may supplement the advice they receive from officials by seeking on a purely informal basis other advice from outside specialists and experts. For example, Anthony Crosland[11] has explained that because he wanted independent *educational* advice or a check on the advice he was getting from his officials, and because he wanted it from people whose sympathies were Labour, he had two groups of people, one for schools and one for higher education, who used to meet periodically in his home – and these groups were specifically to discuss ideas (compared with departmental officials whose work it was to administer). It is rarely a question of which is the right way of soliciting such advice, it is more often a question of accepting, as one of the facts of governmental life, that such advice will be sought, then raising questions about the comparative values of the various advice. There is a fundamental difference of quality between the brainstorming sessions held by Crosland and the more considered advice gathered together by a more conservative body like an official commission.

Sometimes it may be necessary to establish a commission to focus attention and appreciate a situation, otherwise there is no effective means of ascertaining the views of interest groups on specific suggestions for future policy. Commissions enable outside interests to formulate views and also provide a means for appointing officials to consider matters that may be important but would otherwise be set aside because not sufficiently urgent (the pace of modern government is such that some officials rarely have time to consider what is important, only what is urgent).

Also, commission recommendations may subsequently constitute a basis for future work of fundamental importance lasting several years – thus much subsequent detail can be, on occasions, traced to specific commission reports, and without the reports and the acceptance of their recommendations there are sometimes insufficient resources to achieve even highly esteemed objectives.

One of the values of a commission – at least in the opinion of those sympathetic to reforms within the system of government – is to give a push to the official bureaucracy to begin reform activities. This is done partly in the specific recommendations that may be contained in the report, but perhaps more importantly, by breaking the ice so that changes, including those not previously mentioned at all, become discussable. Thus commissions not only have the role of appreciating a situation, they also on occasions create a climate for action. They are, as Sir Geoffrey Vickers has said, not only analytic but catalytic.[12]

In terms of analysing their effectiveness one returns to the somewhat unoriginal generalisation that has occurred again and again in this book. So much depends on objectives – the objectives of those setting up the commission as well as the objectives of the members both individually and collectively. The heyday of Royal Commissions seems to have been over a hundred years ago and there is no longer such a need for committees of wise laymen who can with a degree of leisure consider a problem area. In the more quickly moving twentieth century system of public administration there may instead be a need for inquiries undertaken by much smaller committees of experts and for advisory bodies constituted on entirely different bases. There is certainly need for greater precision of thought about the intended and conceived objectives of all commissions.

Over half a century ago the Haldane Committee on the Machinery of Government made recommendations which seem as relevant today as when they were first made. The Committee reported:

'. . . we have come to the conclusion, after surveying what came before us, that in the sphere of civil government the duty of investigation and thought, as a preliminary to action, might with great advantage be more definitely recognised. It appears to us that adequate provision has not been made in the past for the organised acquisition of facts and information, and for the systematic application of thought, as preliminary to the settlement of policy and its subsequent administration.'[13]

After fifty years of development in the social sciences we seem in this respect to have made little progress.

NOTES

1 See Report of the Departmental Committee on the Procedure of Royal Commissions, HMSO, Cd. 5235, 1910, especially para. 24. This power of commissions normally appointed at the will and discretion of the executive government may be contrasted with that of Select Committees, which are appointed by either House of Parliament, or Tribunals of Inquiry under the

Tribunals of Inquiry (Evidence) Act: any coercive jurisdiction which might be possible in these cases is exercised, not by the particular body but by Parliament which appointed it and the courts which serve it.

2 K. C. Wheare, *Government by Committee*, Oxford University Press, 1955.

3 H. McD. Clokie and J. William Robinson, *Royal Commissions of Inquiry: The Significance of Investigations in British Politics*, Stanford University Press, 1937, p. 157.

4 *The Civil Service*, Vol. 1, Report of the Committee 1966–1968, HMSO, Cmnd. 3638, 1968, Appendix A.

5 Report of the Departmental Committee on the Procedure of Royal Commissions, para. 15.

6 F. F. Ridley (Ed.), *Specialists and Generalists: A Comparative Study of the Professional Civil Servant at Home and Abroad*, Allen & Unwin, 1968.

7 See Sir Geoffrey Vickers, *The Art of Judgement: A Study of Policy-Making*, Chapman & Hall, 1965.

8 See Clokie and Robinson, op. cit.

9 Ibid. p. v.

10 Sir Arthur Salter, Preface in R. V. Vernon and N. Mansergh (Eds,). *Advisory Bodies, A Study of their Uses in Relation to Central Government 1919–1939*, George Allen & Unwin, 1940, p. 7.

11 Edward Boyle and Anthony Crosland in conversation with Maurice Kogan, *The Politics of Education*, Penguin, 1971, p. 185.

12 Sir Geoffrey Vickers, op. cit. p. 50.

13 Report of the Machinery of Government Committee, HMSO, Cd. 9230, 1918, para. 12.

Appendix

The full references for the reports discussed in this symposium are:

THE FULTON COMMITTEE ON THE CIVIL SERVICE
The Civil Service, Vol. 1, Report of the Committee, 1966–68; Vol. 2, Report of the Management Consultancy Group; Vol. 3, Surveys and Investigations; Vol. 4, Factual, statistical and explanatory papers; Vol. 5, Proposals and opinions Cmnd. 3638, HMSO, 1968–69.

THE DONOVAN ROYAL COMMISSION ON TRADE UNIONS
Royal Commission on Trade Unions and Employers' Associations 1965–68 Report, Cmnd. 3623, HMSO, 1968.

THE PLOWDEN COMMITTEE ON PRIMARY EDUCATION
Children and their Primary Schools. A Report of the Central Advisory Council for Education (England); Vol. 1, The Report, Vol. 2, Research and Surveys, HMSO, 1967.

THE REDCLIFFE–MAUD ROYAL COMMISSION ON LOCAL GOVERNMENT
Report of the Royal Commission on Local Government in England, 1966–1969, Vol. 1, Report, Vol. 2, Memorandum of Dissent by Mr D. Senior, Vol. 3, Research Appendices, Cmnd. 4040, HMSO, 1969.
('Also Local Government Reform': Short Version of the Report, Cmnd. 4039).

THE SEEBOHM COMMITTEE ON PERSONAL SOCIAL SERVICES
Report of the Committee on Local Authority and Allied Personal Social Services, Cmnd. 3703, HMSO, 1968.

Index

Numbers in italic indicate Notes

parental participation, policy for advocated in Plowden Report, 94, 99

parish councils, 115, 125, 126

parish government, little knowledge on, 123

Parker, Julia, research for Plowden Committee, 93

Parker, Julia and Allen, Rosalind, on lack of generalised professional goals among social workers, 146

Parker, R. A., 151, 152, 153, 154

parliamentary questions, 27, 82, 87

Peaker, Gilbert, 86, 93

Permanent Secretaries, 22, 28, 32, 89, 112

personal social services, 125, 130, 143–44, 149, 150, 153, 155, 159, 160, 163, 164, 167, 169, 171

personnel management, in the Civil Service, 23, 27

proposals of Fulton Committee on, 29–31, 33–34

Peters, R. S., criticism of Plowden Committee, 92

Pickering, J. F., on Civil Service unsuccessfuls, 20

Plowden, Lady, 9, 83, 89, 90, 92, 99, 152

Plowden Committee, 155, 180, 181

and the machinery of government, 100–2

membership of, 90–91, 95, 96, 101, 179, 180

methods of work, 90–95, 180

pressures for and against, 87–90

secretarial assistance, 91, 92, 93, 94, 101

terms of reference of, 82, 91, 179, 180

Plowden Report (*Children and their Primary Schools*, Report of the Central Advisory Council for Education (England), Vols.

1–2, 1967), 81, 84, 86, 87, 164

effects of, 98–100

reaction to, 98–99

recommendations of, 85, 94, 95–96, 96–98, 99–100

research for, 93–95, *103*, 177, 180, 183

Political Quarterly, article by Derek Senior on local government, 112

Pollock, Sir George, 74

'positive discrimination', advocated by Plowden Committee, 86–87, 94, 96, 98–99

Power, Michael, work for the Seebohm Committee, 157

'preference for relevance' in the selection of administrators, 37

Prentice, Reginald, 148

Prices and Incomes Acts, 75

Priestley Royal Commission on the Civil Service, 1953–55, 13, 26

primary education, 82, 88, 91, 92, 94, 96

primary schools, 88, 94, 96, 97, 98, 100

Principal Executive Officers, 34

Principals, 21, 33, 34, 91, 153

principle, definition of, 111

principles, for local government reform, 110, *141*, 116, 122, 123–24, 132–34

probation service, 144, 147, 150, 155, 156, 160–61, 168

procedure agreements, 53, 61, 62, 67

productivity agreements, 65

productivity bargaining, 55, 57, 59, 64

Professional and Technology Category, formed, 34

Professional Works Group, 21, 26

Profile of a Profession: the Administrative Class of the Civil Service, by R. A. Chapman (Vol. 3 (2) of the Fulton Report), 18, 20